OVERCOMING REDUNDANCY

52 INSPIRING IDEAS TO HELP YOU BOUNCE BACK FROM LOSING YOUR JOB

D1337328

GORDON ADAMS

infiniteideas

First published in 2009 by
Infinite Ideas Limited
36 St Giles
Oxford, OX1 3LD
United Kingdom
www.infideas.com

A CIP catalogue record for this book is available from the British Library

ISBN 978–1–906821–26–5

Cover designed by Baseline Arts Ltd, Oxford
Typeset by Sparks, Oxford – www.sparkspublishing.com
Printed and bound in Great Britain by Clays Ltd, St Ives PLC

TECHNICAL NOTE ABOUT
THE REDUNDANCY TRANSFORMATIONS STUDY

The Redundancy Transformations Study was a nationally representative online survey of 1,004 adults aged 18 and over who had experienced redundancy during their working lives. It was carried out by Alternative Futures Research Ltd in February and March 2009. The online sample was provided by Toluna. An earlier pilot phase of this research comprising 147 online interviews was also carried out with the help of One Life Live. Where respondents from this research survey are quoted in this book, names have been changed to protect their identities.

For more information contact Alternative Futures Research Ltd
www.alternativefutures.biz

CONTENTS

Foreword   viii

Introduction: The view from both sides of the fence   ix

1   Be positive   1

2   Stay on good terms with your former employer   4

3   Consider your options   8

4   Be friends with change   11

5   Stay active   14

6   Network with friends and relatives   17

7   Make new connections   20

8   Do a good turn for someone else   24

9   Don't be afraid   27

10   Leave bitterness behind   29

11   Ask yourself the right questions   33

12   Retrain for a new career   35

13   Increase your skill set   39

14   Take voluntary work   42

15   Fulfil a lifelong ambition   45

16   Recharge your batteries   47

17   Carry out a skills audit on yourself   49

18   Redraft your CV   52

19   Register with recruitment consultants   55

20   Market yourself online   58

21   Practise your elevator speech   61

22   Research other careers   64

23   Seek career guidance   67

24 Invest your redundancy money wisely 71
25 Follow your passion 75
26 Use an interim solution as a stepping stone 78
27 Make looking for work your work 80
28 Go freelance 83
29 Set up your own business as a sole trader 86
30 Set up your own business as a partnership or limited company 89
31 Invest in a franchise 93
32 Close the book 97
33 Reassess your priorities in life 99
34 Give yourself a fresh image 102
35 Find your inner calm 105
36 Practise your interview technique 108
37 Be focused 111
38 Write a book 114
39 Set your finances in order 118
40 Obtain a grant or funding 122
41 Create a new routine 125
42 Choose an alternative lifestyle 128
43 Go back to school or university 132
44 Listen to others who've been there before 135
45 Work abroad 138
46 Find inspiration 141
47 Enrol with a coach 144
48 Set up your own support group 147
49 Create a portfolio career 150
50 Downshift your life 153
51 Enjoy time with your family 155
52 Believe in yourself! 157

Appendix: Useful contacts 160
Other helpful books from Infinite Ideas 163
Index 165

FOREWORD

We live in challenging times. Over the coming years more than a million people in the UK are likely to lose their jobs as a result of problems affecting the global economy. Redundancy is becoming a common part of modern life. Around one in four adults currently experiences redundancy in their lifetime and this figure appears likely to rise.

Redundancy is nothing to be ashamed of, it is a transition phase to the next stage of your career and it is something to be faced up to.

At Penna, we help tens of thousands of managers each year with their career transition decisions whether it is finding their next role, starting up a business, or indeed a portfolio career. We see at close quarters the emotional and practical impacts of redundancy and the effect it can have on a person's self-confidence and career plans. We encourage people to think things through and develop their ideas in one-to-one coaching sessions and workshops. People come to see their situation as an opportunity, not a problem. We help them discover the best path.

We believe this book will help those who have been recently affected by redundancy to prepare and move forward. Anyone who reads it is likely to come away with at least a few ideas they haven't thought of before. This book will provide them with ideas which they can develop with their families, friends and professional advisers. It will help them begin to move forwards with their lives again.

I wish you good luck with your future career.

Bev White
Managing Director Transition Services
Penna

INTRODUCTION: THE VIEW FROM BOTH SIDES OF THE FENCE

To paraphrase an old Joni Mitchell song, 'I've looked at this from both sides now, from win and lose'.

My own story, taking in the twenty-five years of my working life so far, includes two different experiences of redundancy. Once I was a survivor: I stayed while the company downsized and most of my colleagues were made redundant all around me. Once I suffered redundancy: I took the package on offer and used the money start up my own business. That proved to be the best decision of my working life. I'm convinced that there is no winning side and no losing side with redundancy. It's what you make of it that counts.

To stay in a company that has been making severe job cuts is not a pleasant experience. I found it emotionally difficult. I lost colleagues that I counted as friends, people I'd enjoyed working with. I felt guilty that I had somehow escaped the axe while people I knew to be talented professionals had lost their jobs. I felt bitter – not a clever reaction, and one that I now regret – about the way the company had acted. I felt disillusioned. The working side of the business fell into chaos for several months in the aftermath of what were quite savage cuts. It was not a pleasant place to work. The staff that remained were demotivated.

I noticed something very strange, though – something that I now know is not unusual. The people who left because of redundancy 'moved on' in their lives. After a while they found new jobs, sometimes in completely new directions. Some moved home. Some found temporary employment before finding a permanent role. Some started their own businesses. They seemed happier than before. On the other hand, some of the people who stayed, myself included, did not move on in any sense. We were stuck in the same jobs as before, in a company that some of us no longer wanted to work for. Feeling that way, I applied for new jobs and eventually found my own way out of the exit door, not a moment too soon.

Many years later in my career, I had the opposite experience. My company had restructured and my part of the company had been taken over by another firm. Job cuts were expected by everyone as the two organisations merged. A friend of mine in the HR department encouraged me to seek redundancy. I asked for redundancy as it would certainly have occurred anyway, but it felt at last like I was taking control of my life. I was given a good redundancy payment that I used to help me to start my own business. I received excellent outplacement support through Penna, where a small business coach helped me through the early stages of establishing my own business. I will always be grateful for that expert help.

With help and advice from others, I was able to overcome redundancy. Now I'm happier in my working life than I ever was before. With the right attitude and with the right help, I am sure you will bounce back too. Good luck in all you decide to do. I hope some of the ideas in this book will strike a chord with you and help you on your way.

Gordon Adams
May 2009

The author wishes to thank the following organisations for their assist-ance with this book:

- Penna plc
- One Life Events Ltd. (One Life Live)
- Alternative Futures Research Ltd.

Thanks also to all the organisations and individuals who have helped by providing case studies, expert comment or other practical assistance in the creation of this book.

1 BE POSITIVE

Good things happen to positive people. You can make the breaks as well as take them. You'll find it easier to find a new job if you react positively to this challenge. A new employer is more likely to take you on if they can see how well you responded to this blow.

You have just been made redundant – so how do you feel? Angry, bitter, rejected, disbelieving, sad, disappointed, cynical, uncertain, anxious, fearful?

The one word that probably doesn't sum up how you're feeling right now is POSITIVE. Yet that's what those who have successfully overcome redundancy say is the most important thing of all: staying positive.

So how can you make yourself think positively?

Try thinking about things in a different way. See this moment as an opportunity. You have now got a once-in-a-lifetime opportunity to reassess your career. Were you really enjoying it fully? Was it fulfilling? Was it using all your skills to best advantage? Did you go to work each morning with a spring in your step? If not, you've just been given the chance to change. Today could be the day you take your first step in a new career direction.

Think positively about yourself. What skills have you picked up in your working life? What can you do now that you couldn't do when you first started work? Where else could that knowledge be put to use? Think about the skills that could be redeployed. The next job you do might not be in the same industry or same job role as before.

Being made redundant could turn out to be a big break for you. If you are fortunate enough to receive a substantial sum of money as a redundancy payment, now is the time to move your life forwards. Find a new job before that money is spent and you'll have succeeded. Invest the money wisely to bring future gain – for instance, spending it on retraining for a new career, starting your own business or buying a franchise to run an established business – and you'll be a winner.

Remember this: every challenge is also an opportunity. You have the opportunity to invest your time and your redundancy money to bring about the future life that you want.

Be aware how common this experience is. In the UK, approximately one person in every four will experience redundancy at some point in their working lives. Major moments – when the whole direction of a person's life turns around – are sometimes referred to as Pivot Points. After starting a relationship, divorce, the birth of children and the death of loved ones, redundancy is the most important single life-changing experience according to research by Alternative Futures in 2008 into Pivot Points. Two out of every three people whose life is changed by redundancy see their lives changed for the better, according to research by the same company. The Redundancy Transformations Study in 2009 revealed that over half of people who experience redundancy ultimately come to view it as the *best thing that ever happened to them*! This experience typically prompts people to make some major changes in their lives, changes that turn out in time to have been for the best.

> *'People who have successfully overcome redundancy say it is crucial to stay positive – yet one in three admits to feeling bitter or angry at the time.'*
> REDUNDANCY TRANSFORMATIONS STUDY, ALTERNATIVE FUTURES, 2009

Don't take this redundancy personally. Redundancy is *not* your fault. I often refer, in this book, to *people* 'being made redundant', but this is simply a reflection of the way we normally talk. It's not actually the case. It was the job role that was no longer needed. It was the job that was made redundant – *not* you.

You can't always choose what happens to you in life. But you can choose your response – so choose to be positive!

The rise and fall of employment in particular industry sectors is inevitable. When whole economies have difficulties, when industries experience a downturn, when items fall out of fashion, when established products are displaced by the next technological advance, then redundancies almost inevitably follow. You just have to resolve to go with the flow, wherever life takes you.

It is up to you to choose your response to this situation. You have the ability to choose how you will react to this. You can choose to be negative, cynical, disenchanted and disheartened. Or you can choose to be positive and believe in yourself. You can see this as a chance you have been given – and resolve to emerge stronger as a result. Being positive is the first step to overcoming redundancy. If you're willing to take that step, then read on.

2 STAY ON GOOD TERMS WITH YOUR FORMER EMPLOYER

Stay on good terms with your former employer. You still need them for a reference in future. People still employed there might help you over the years to come. Your paths may cross again someday.

How do you feel about your former employer right now? Your answer may not be printable. But it is important for you to leave bitterness behind. You need to avoid sounding angry, cynical and disillusioned.

'Just 71% of people made redundant say they left on good terms with their former employer – many more now wish they had.'
REDUNDANCY TRANSFORMATIONS STUDY, ALTERNATIVE FUTURES, 2009

The way to a better life and a new job is through accepting what has happened and moving on. It will be helpful for you simply to accept that your employer was a victim of economic boom and bust, of market fluctuations, of changing patterns of consumer demand. Your employer did not *want* to make you redundant, it *needed* to. That's just part of business life. It wasn't personal; it was an economic decision. So don't take it personally. Make a point of forgiving your former employer and moving on.

Redundancy has been compared by some experts to bereavement. You experience the same process of grief. Typically you move through several different phases: from a sense of loss and shock, through denial ('This can't be happening to me'), into anger and other emotional reactions until finally you reach the point of acceptance where you can begin rebuilding your life. You have a strong interest in moving as swiftly as you can through these different phases, reaching this end point as quickly as possible. Because it is only then that you can begin anew.

So why is it a good idea to stay on good terms with your former employer? Well, for a start, you need them to give you a good reference in the future. You have a vested interest in biting your tongue and staying on good terms with them. But there is more. Unless the company you worked for is closing down completely, your former employer (and the people who still work there) may be part of your future in some way. Many of your friends may still be working there now. Some will probably move on in the next year or two. If you react well and in future they are in a position to help you, they might be disposed to do so. You may still be working in the same industry in your next job and your paths may cross again. Here's the worst case: imagine how you'd feel if your next job was working for a *supplier* that suddenly wants to sell its products or services to your former *employer*? If you've spoken out of turn to your previous employer, this could become a very uncomfortable situation for you. If you've stayed on good terms and conducted yourself with dignity, it's easier. So bite your tongue and overcome your negativity. Stay above the fray. Be as pleasant as you can possibly be to your former employer and any former colleagues who still work there. It is not easy coping with redundancy: you need to deal with feelings of rejection and bitterness. But nor is it easy being one of those who stay behind whilst those around them are made redundant. They need to deal with their 'survivor guilt', the loss of good friends and colleagues and (quite probably) an increase in workload. Make it easier for them by showing yourself to be big enough to conquer your own negativity and move on.

'It's very difficult but very important to have an elegant exit. It's a very small world out there and your paths may cross again. Also many references will be taken over the telephone where what is not said can sometimes be more important than what is said.'
KATE FARRINGTON, PRINCIPAL CAREER CONSULTANT, PENNA

STAYING ON GOOD TERMS – A CASE STUDY

Ros Lund was happily employed at American Express for more than nine years, firstly as a Process Manager and later as a Sales Strategy Director. Her role became redundant following a major company restructuring. The company decided to move from a European to an international structure. She was put on a month's consultation with a further 90 days' notice while the company sought alternative positions for her. She was also given outplacement support through Penna at this time. Ros was fortunate: before the consultation period ended she managed to secure a six-month secondment within the Business Travel section, so didn't actually leave the company at this point. However, the threat of redundancy hadn't been removed – she had gained six months' breathing space. The outplacement counselling she received while her job was under threat set her thinking. Other people in AmEx were coming up to her and asking for advice on their CVs and careers. She found she enjoyed giving this kind of help. Ros decided that in the long-term she would like to retrain as an Executive Coach.

She took a free 'taster' weekend with the Coaching Academy, one of the biggest coaching organisations in the UK. Then she persuaded American Express to fund her taking the Diploma in Corporate and Executive Coaching. 'The company was actually quite keen to get an experienced director on secondment,' Ros recalls, 'so they agreed to let me incorporate coaching skills into the role.' So over the next year – as the six-month secondment was extended to a full year – Ros and an external coach trained more than one hundred managers across the company in coaching skills. Eventually the secondment came to an end and she took redundancy in the summer of 2008. This was over a year after the original internal announcement that her role had been made redundant. She has since gone on to set up her own coaching business, Fresh Lens Coaching, and also continues to work with Penna, the company that gave her outplacement support.

She is pleased that throughout the redundancy process she remained on good terms with her employer. It enabled her to obtain training for a new career, at her employer's expense, while inching towards the exit. 'I feel it is vitally important to stay on good terms with your employer,' she says. 'It can be hard. You can feel quite bruised when you're made redundant, but you've really got to rise above it. You never know when you might *like* to work with them, or *need* to work with them, in future.' Ros has also worked with American Express again since starting her own coaching business. 'I've worked with them indirectly since setting up my own business. And I'm still having coffees regularly with many of the people I worked with at AmEx. Hopefully we'll work together again in the future.'

3 CONSIDER YOUR OPTIONS

Redundancy is an opportunity to take stock of where you are and where you want to go. Take time to consider your options and don't rush to judgement.

Redundancy is a big challenge but it is also an opportunity. If this is happening to you mid-career, you now have a once-in-a-lifetime opportunity to take stock of where you are in your life and compare it to where you really want to be.

'A wise man will make more opportunities than he finds.'
FRANCIS BACON

Don't rush to judgement here. Too many people return unthinkingly to 'more of the same'. If you hated your previous job, if it wasn't motivating you, or if it wasn't using your full range of skills and abilities, maybe now is the time for a change?

You have a wide range of options at this point.

- Perhaps it is time to switch from full-time to part-time work, and get a better work-life balance?
- Perhaps a variety of temporary or contract work would be more stimulating and allow you to try out different sectors of employment to find what's right for you?
- Perhaps it is time to break free and be your own boss by setting up your own business, going into partnership with someone else, working as a freelancer or buying a business franchise?

- Perhaps you should invest your time and redundancy money into retraining for a new career?

- Perhaps it is time to return to school or university in order to acquire new knowledge?

- Perhaps it is time to move to another part of the country to improve your employment prospects?

- Perhaps it is time to downshift your life by moving to a smaller or cheaper home and making do with less?

- Or perhaps it is simply time to take a break – to travel the world, write a book, or achieve some other life goal that you've never had time for before?

The options are many and varied. But how can you choose between them? How can you know which is the right course of action for you?

Here's a suggestion for you. Set aside a full day for this task because it is really important.

Start by making a list of *all* your options. This book will hopefully give you a few ideas. Be open-minded and make this list of options as long as possible. Try to include at least one item on this list that is something you've always dreamed of doing, even if you don't think it is realistic or achievable. For instance, if you've got a passion for cars, gardening, antiques, music or art, try to include an option that taps into that passion in some way.

Now write down next to each option a list of all the reasons why it appeals to you, and all of the reasons it doesn't appeal. For instance you might write down 'Take an interim management or temporary job in the same industry as before.'

'No great man ever complains of want of opportunity.'
RALPH WALDO EMERSON

This option might appeal because it gets you back into work quickly and brings in money. It might not appeal because it involves a great deal of commuting to a new location and doesn't move your career immediately further forward. Alternatively you might write down 'Start my own business.' This might appeal because it would be exciting, you'd be your own boss and you'd be using the skills you've learned. But it might not appeal because you're scared of the risk of failure and you're really not sure you'd be able to make enough money on your own. Don't reject any idea at this point. Too many good ideas are strangled at birth. You need to nurture them and give them time and space to grow.

After doing this exercise, talk to people you know and trust about your options. Talk to your partner, your family, your former working colleagues and other advisers. Tell them you're mulling over the options and ask their advice. They will probably tell you some things they've noticed about you: where they believe your strengths lie, what things you appear to want or enjoy. This feedback will help you determine your next steps.

If you do this, the way forward will begin to form in your mind. Having a clear vision of what you want to do next in your life is the beginning of making it happen.

4   BE FRIENDS WITH CHANGE

One thing is certain in the days ahead: your life is going to change. It is no use fighting this. Make a decision now to embrace change and to make that change work for you.

When major changes happen in people's lives we often see them struggling to accept it. Whether it is a relationship breakdown, a major health problem or even bereavement, the same characteristic response is there to be seen. We hear ourselves saying, 'They are in denial.'

Well, today it may be you who is in denial. You may still be looking backwards, not forwards. You may still be going over recent events in your mind, rather than looking to the future and the change that is upon you. You may be being self-indulgent, allowing yourself to go over events time and time again in your mind, rather than looking at what you can do now to move your life forwards.

'Only 38% of people who are made redundant return to exactly the same type of work they did before.' REDUNDANCY TRANSFORMATIONS STUDY, ALTERNATIVE FUTURES, 2009

The one undeniable thing is that your life is about to change. Most people who are made redundant do not go back to a job that is exactly the same as the one they left. Most choose a new path: for instance, a different type of job, becoming self-employed, a period of academic study or retraining, or early retirement.

'It's not the strongest that survive, or the most intelligent but the ones most responsive to change.'

CHARLES DARWIN

It will be harder for you to accept change if you were in your previous job or with your previous employer for a very long time. This makes the redundancy more akin to a divorce. To a large extent, that employment may have defined your life. You may feel it included some of the best years of your life. You will inevitably have feelings of sadness and of rejection. But you are now free. It's down to you to make the most of that freedom to carve out a new direction for yourself, one that will bring out the very best in you.

BEING FRIENDS WITH CHANGE – A CASE STUDY

Ian had more than twenty years of service with a well-known financial services company. He was made redundant in 2005 at the age of 53.

It was a big shock for Ian to find himself back on the jobs market after all this time. Ian knew also that his age could make it difficult for him to find a new job quickly. One thing he felt particularly strongly was that it was time for a change. He decided he wanted to change to a new sector.

At first, recruitment agencies pushed him towards jobs in financial services and other sectors where he had prior experience. He was advised to take customer relationship management roles similar to those he had done before. He resisted the pressure to get a new job quickly and gave up time to redrafting his CV and to various assessments of the things he enjoyed most in a job. This led to identification of potential new directions for him.

The hard work paid off. Aspects of work that were particularly appealing to Ian included project work, handling business challenges and international travel. He has now gained a job with a major international healthcare organisation where he has responsibility for international expansion of a particular division of the company. He has managed a major acquisition for them in Australia and travelled to a wide variety of global destinations in Europe and the Americas to assess potential acquisition targets.

It has proved to be a good move for Ian and he's pleased he didn't leap back immediately into 'more of the same'.

Ian's advice for others is simple. 'Treat the redundancy as an opportunity to expand your experience by moving into a new sector. Be friends with change. Understand yourself clearly: be clear what elements would be required for your perfect job. Then stay focused and patient and you'll get there in the end.'

5 STAY ACTIVE

Give yourself tasks each day that will get you out of bed in the mornings. Don't let your 'get up and go' just get up and go! Keep on the move. Make sure each new day brings something new. Don't let yourself slow down or opt out.

It's all too easy after you've been made redundant to simply slow down. Face it, you've gone from having a fully organised, totally constrained 9 to 5 – and admit it, it was really more of an 8 to 7, wasn't it? – to having each day as a blank sheet of paper. If you allow yourself to succumb, inactivity not activity will become the norm.

Each day needs to feel like it is taking you one step closer to a new job. At the end of each day, you should be able to look back on it and say you did something that moved your next employment closer.

It may be a very small thing, for instance making a phone call or meeting up with a former working colleague. It might be sending a speculative email or registering with a new recruitment website. It may be developing yourself, by starting to read a book on a personal development subject or enquiring about a training course. Or it may be making a shopping trip to invest in a new outfit to wear at job interviews. These are all small steps on the road to hearing about new job opportunities, upskilling yourself, improving your image and making yourself more employable.

'Keep active' must be your watchword. Don't let your energy level drop. You need to make things happen, not lie back and wait for them to happen to you.

Here are some tips on ways you can stay active. Choose at least one of these and decide to adopt it.

Start each day (before or after breakfast depending on your preference) with some exercise: a brisk walk or cycle ride, jogging in your local park or a visit to the gym. All these activities give you a burst of adrenaline. They all provide you with at least half an hour's thinking time. The truth is you will think better and your mind will be clearer if you have been active. If you do this, thoughts about jobs and careers will begin to fall into place.

Help a friend or neighbour – or a local good cause – with a task. Even if this is something as small as babysitting for someone you know, walking their dog, delivering leaflets or painting a fence, you will be developing your contacts, doing something to help you feel good about yourself and keeping your personal energy setting on high.

> *'Our greatest glory is not in never falling, but in rising every time we fall.'*
> CONFUCIUS

Make a list of the things you need to do (or want to do) and try to accomplish at least one task each day. This might include all the household DIY tasks you've never had time to do before. Admit it, it wasn't time but inclination that was lacking, wasn't it? Now you've a chance to get them out of the way. After you achieve this, you will enjoy the sense of accomplishment that comes from completing a task that you didn't really want to do. You'll have that sense of being virtuous. You'll feel in control. You will have had feeding time for your self-esteem!

Sort out your paperwork and get your financial affairs into good order. Bring all your financial paperwork (bank statements, mortgage statements, insurance policies and so on) together in one place. Review your financial situation carefully. If you haven't already done so, put all your monthly outgoings onto a spreadsheet, together with any regular income your household is receiving. Please don't shrink from this task. You know you need to face up to it. If you get to grips with your household finances, you'll know exactly how long your funds will last, you'll know how big the financial challenge is that you are facing. If you understand the situation, you can begin to plan, not begin to panic.

Join a group. This can be anything from a sports or social club, networking group or group of volunteers for a local charity. Get out of the house and meet people. Offer to help them in some way and they may be able to help you in return. I am not suggesting beginning to act as if you are in early retirement, or that your focus should be diverted from the search for a new job. What I am suggesting is that the more activity there is in your life, the greater the drive you display, the happier you'll be and the easier you'll find it to get another job.

So whatever you do, stay active! Sleep and rest is important – you may need to recharge your batteries at first – but oversleep and lethargy, and the despondency they can provoke, are your enemies. Get up (each morning), stay up (mentally), keep up (with all the tasks you've set yourself) and upwards is the direction your life will go!

6 NETWORK WITH FRIENDS AND RELATIVES

This is a time in your life when support from friends and relatives is going to be particularly important to you. Make sure you seek out their company and accept their advice and help.

Networking with friends (including former working colleagues) and relatives may move you closer to your next job.

It's vital to stay active and connect with others. In some cases, this word should perhaps be 'reconnect'. Look up your old friends again – seek out some of your more distant relatives and acquaintances that you haven't had time to see for a long while.

Your friends and relatives have a double role to play. Firstly, they can act as a support network to help you bounce back. You are human, so your confidence will undoubtedly have taken a knock as a result of this redundancy. You need the support and encouragement of your friends and relatives to remind you of all the things you can do. They believe in you – you just need to reaffirm your belief in yourself!

Your friends and relatives can also help you to find a new job. They can be your 'eyes and ears' everywhere they go. It's an obvious thing to say

'Networking is crucial, though a lot of people are resistant to the idea at first. Those who are open-minded soon see the benefit of using networking to access the large unadvertised jobs market.'

KATE FARRINGTON, PRINCIPAL CAREER CONSULTANT, PENNA

'One person in every four finds their next job following redundancy via networking. For senior managers, this figure rises to one in three.'

REDUNDANCY TRANSFORMATIONS STUDY, ALTERNATIVE FUTURES, 2009

but to get a new job you need to hear about it and a prospective employer needs to hear about you.

Consider this for a moment: Think of those among your good friends or close relatives who are in a job at the moment. Think of the organisations that employ them. How many employers does that give you some kind of a connection with? Let's say the answer is fifty. If your friends and relatives stay alert on your behalf, they can tip you off about any jobs that are going with the companies they work for. So you have perhaps fifty employers 'under surveillance'. For these fifty employers you would hope to hear quickly about any new job opportunities for which you were suitable.

But let's assume your friends and relatives are even more active than that. As a result of speaking to you they are fully informed and energised on your behalf. They are now actively looking for new opportunities for you. Because they've spoken recently to you they know exactly what kind of new job you are looking for. So they don't just keep tabs on job opportunities with their own employer, they also talk about you and your situation to all their friends. Whenever they get the chance, they talk about you and mention the kind of job you are looking for. Now how many connections do you have? You won't just connect with your friends' employers but the employers of everyone they know. Do the maths. Now you might have indirect connections with $50 \times 50 = 2500$ employers. If you network actively, you can potentially be alerted about job opportunities with several thousand different employers.

Many of the job opportunities you will hear about via networking are never advertised.

I need to make clear that I'm extending the word 'friends' here to include former working colleagues and business contacts. Many managers are initially cynical about the idea of building and maintaining a professional network. But we've all heard the adage 'it's not what you know, it's who you know' that gets you into a job. One of the main things you have gained from all of the years of your working life is a pool of contacts who you know and trust, and who know and trust you. Choose the people among them who you like and respect – get back in contact with them. As Jon, a former company executive, explains: 'I've learned how important it is to use your network! I didn't realise the power of my network. People told me it was the best way to get a job, but I thought I knew better. Using your network, judiciously and sensibly, will pay huge dividends. And once you have the new job, keep up the networking, as you – or others – may need it in the future.'

Networking works! Make sure it works for you.

7 MAKE NEW CONNECTIONS

Actively seek out new connections with people you hadn't previously known. Take up offers of introductions. Join networking groups.

Successful networking is about reawakening old connections and making new connections. If you look up all your old friends and former work colleagues, you will have a ready pool of contacts to speak to.

Make sure you reconnect with those you particularly liked and respected. Social networking websites can help you do this. There are many good networking websites around like Friends Reunited (for old school friends) and LinkedIn or Plaxo (for former work colleagues, helping you find out where they are now so you can get back in contact). Every contact you make will inevitably throw up an 'Are you still in contact with Paul or Kate?' moment. Have they heard about what a former colleague is doing these days? This kind of discussion can lead to reconnections with other people that you have lost touch with. Each expansion of your contact pool may bring you closer to your next job. Meeting up with old contacts can also be a lot of fun along the way!

Making totally new connections is very important too. This doesn't have to be a complete cold call. If someone you know offers to introduce you to someone else who they think can help you, go along with this. Take up their kind offer and make that connection happen!

If you are thinking of starting up your own business, there are many networking events you can attend. In the early days of thinking whether or not to become self-employed, you'll probably be meeting like-minded people at seminars run by Business Link or your bank. Most major towns have a variety of breakfast, lunch and evening networking gatherings for the business community. These are organised by everyone from the local Chamber of Commerce and professional bodies through to commercial networking organisations like BNI (Business Network International) or BRX (Business Referral Exchange). Some networking organisations organise for their members to meet locally once a week, over a meal, and swap contacts. It's the 'you help me and I'll help you in return' principle.

Networking helps you to take back the initiative in your life. You can make opportunities happen!

You can usually attend one meeting initially as a non-member. You may not even have started your own business formally yet – for instance, you might simply be looking for some freelance work to tide you over – but you can still go along to these kinds of meetings. Some mistakenly expect them to be formal, intimidating affairs. They aren't – they're just another way of making connections. Look to help the people you encounter. If you can do someone else a favour, they may return the favour. You will generally find, as a rule of thumb, that you need to meet someone face-to-face on at least three occasions to begin to establish that person as a helpful networking contact. They won't instantly

Get out and tell the world what you do!

feel comfortable enough with you or familiar enough with your experience to refer you to others. So don't expect instant results. You have to work hard to develop mutual understanding and trust.

Be open to new connections at off-duty moments. In the case study that follows, Caroline made a particularly important business connection on holiday. This is not about shameless self-promotion or never switching off and relaxing! It is simply about being yourself and telling people openly about yourself and your plans whenever you meet them. It is also about not seeing people in a fixed way. In Caroline's story, a supplier at one point in her life became her employer at another.

MAKING NEW CONNECTIONS – A CASE STUDY

Caroline was Head of Marketing for a financial services company. She had been with the same company for more than fifteen years but felt she was getting stale in her job. She says of the time, 'I wasn't getting a buzz out of going in to work each day. The company had changed so much and many of the people I enjoyed working with the most had moved on. I knew I wanted to do something different, something more exciting, but wasn't really sure what.'

After speaking to some of her friends and family she decided to seek voluntary redundancy. 'I was in a comfortable enough position financially. A redundancy cheque would enable me to pay off my mortgage. I knew I could take the risk of earning less for a few years. So I decided to go freelance.' This move would also allow her to work from home and have a better work-life balance. It left more time for amateur dramatics, her private passion. So she set up her own marketing consultancy business as a sole trader. Through a friend, she also found an initial interim management position for six months in London working two days a week. 'This was the best of both worlds: I had a secure income coming in from the interim management role and at the same time I had several days a week free to develop my own business.'

Her most surprising finding? 'I found out that from small acorns unusual oaks can grow. Networking with different people sometimes produced the most unlikely results.' For instance, her interim management work helped her in her freelance role. 'I met a website designer through the interim management job. He helped to design our company website. We became firm friends. He has since asked me to head up a new division of his company, offering training on website content management. When I was in the corporate world, I'd never have thought of going into the website design business in a million years!'

Caroline also found that there's never a bad time to tell other people what you do. 'It's happened so many times for me. One example was when I was on a group holiday and got chatting with some of the people there. It turned out that one of them ran a business offering training to colleges. After the holiday I had a call from her asking me to join her in a tender for a piece of work. We won the business and have been working together ever since.'

8 DO A GOOD TURN FOR SOMEONE ELSE

Self-esteem versus self-pity – that's the battle that's about to be fought. Here's the thing: you need to avoid self-pity and feed your self-esteem. That's why doing a good turn for someone else is the right thing to do right now, just as it always was.

You have time on your hands at the moment. Perhaps not a lot of time – not if you are organising your days, networking, researching your next career move, making job applications and doing some of the other things suggested in this book.

But you have no excuse now to put off jobs that need doing. You've no excuse now not to give aid to someone who needs your help – especially if, in one way or another, it involves using your job skills.

I mean this in its widest sense. In your job you have probably picked up a wide range of skills. You may have picked up skills such as project planning, organisation, time management, managing a budget, managing a team, public speaking, writing persuasively and so on. So when you have a friend or neighbour who needs help writing to their MP, managing a budget for a club they run, organising a charity fund-raiser or who is looking for a speaker for their next club event, there's an obvious candidate, isn't there? You!

You'll feel better for doing it. It will pay dividends in terms of your self-esteem. It will give you a real lift at a time in your life when you need it most.

There's more than just pure altruism at work here. Those you help will want to help you in return. That's natural – it will make them feel good too. If they know about your situation and what kind of a job you're looking for, they can keep their ear to the ground for you. They will do practical things to help you over the coming months if they possibly can. That means a lot. You know where they live and what they do for a living, but you simply don't know (and could never know) the same about all the people they know. It could be a simple act to them to put you in touch with someone they know who retrained mid-career, runs their own business or has retired from the kind of role you are now seeking. All of these helpful acts might result from giving up some time to help them.

Giving your time away sounds foolish, whereas in fact it can be a very practical way to boost your self-esteem at a time when you most need it.

There's an obvious professional move you can make. You can give away some professional days of your time. If you're an accountant or bookkeeper by training, offer to help the treasurer of a local voluntary group. If you used to work in a shop, then volunteer to help your local charity shop. If you're an IT expert, help your neighbours (or anyone you know who works from home) with their PC problems.

One thought is to approach some local employers and offer your time free on a work experience basis. You might offer to act as a mentor or coach to some junior members of their staff, using your business skills. Or offer to do unpaid work for an employer you'd particularly like to work for. This would provide them with evidence of the quality of your work and might lead to further freelance work with them. Could you do something to

'Half of those who have experienced redundancy before would advise others to involve themselves in voluntary, charitable or community work at this time.'

REDUNDANCY TRANSFORMATIONS STUDY, ALTERNATIVE FUTURES, 2009

address a business challenge you know that they face and suggest a way that you might work to assist them?

Check out initiatives such as Time Banks, where people donate an hour of their time to gain a credit that they can then spend to hire someone else for an hour. One hour of your time is valued just the same as an hour of anyone else's. Effectively this is a simple way to swap favours, as no money changes hands. You can feel good about helping other people with everything from gardening and DIY to computer skills or adult literacy – whatever you feel able to offer – while getting some of the help that you need in return. It could be useful if you find, in these economically challenging times, that you've suddenly moved from being cash rich/time poor to cash poor/time rich.

Use your expertise, get out there and help someone!

9 DON'T BE AFRAID

You are at a crossroads now. You can go in any direction you want – it's your choice. The one place you don't want to stay is here and it is only fear that will stop you from moving on. So acknowledge that fear, face up to it, leave your baggage behind and move on.

It's a scary time, isn't it? But not everything that is scary is bad for you. A rollercoaster ride can be scary but exhilarating. The moment you step out of the plane on a parachute jump produces a spike of fear, but you jump anyway.

> *'Courage is resistance to fear, mastery of fear – not absence of fear.'*
> MARK TWAIN

Susan Jeffers, in her excellent book *Feel the Fear and Do It Anyway*, talks of how she learned you need to acknowledge the fear but not let it stop you. Brave people are courageous not because they have no fear. Of course they have fear: they are human like you or I. They feel the fear and face up to it. They overcome it. They feel the fear but still act.

So at this point in your life you may well be nervous, apprehensive or fearful about many things, in particular about your future and the significant changes you might be contemplating:

- Retrain for a new career – at my age?
- Start up my own business – but what if I fail?
- Move home to take a new job – I might not make new friends in a new area!

> *'Pushing through fear is less frightening than living with the underlying fear that comes from a feeling of helplessness.'*
> SUSAN JEFFERS , SELF HELP GURU

- Emigrate to take up a new job overseas – but I can hardly speak the language!
- Apply for a job that is different from what I did before – but what if I can't do the job?
- Invest my redundancy money in buying a business franchise – what if I waste all the money?
- Join the family business – what if I let everyone else down?
- Go to university – but I've never been any good at exams!

Acknowledge these fears. They are all legitimate concerns.

However, if you feel positive about an opportunity; if you have the skills, knowledge and determination to succeed in a particular direction; most of all if you *feel right* about a particular action; then take Susan Jeffers' advice: *feel the fear and do it anyway.*

10 LEAVE BITTERNESS BEHIND

It's time to shed your baggage. Bitterness is one of the things dragging you down and holding you back. Pick it up and throw it overboard!

Being made redundant is not a bittersweet moment. It only leaves a bitter taste. It just proves you are human if you've had any of the following thoughts:

- 'It isn't fair!'
- 'Why me?'
- 'I didn't deserve this kind of treatment.'
- 'They've treated me shoddily.'
- 'The managers here don't know what they're doing.'
- 'I'm better than most of the people they are keeping.'

You can surely add a few more bitter thoughts of your own to this list. All of these thoughts may or may not be true. It really doesn't matter. It has happened and what you think now won't change the past a jot!

What all of these thoughts have in common is the ability to hold you back. They can warp the way you think from day to day. They affect your mood and change the way you react to other people. They hamper your ability to move forward. Perhaps most important of all, if you hold these attitudes, and they eat away at you, you'll bring them into a job interview with you and they will stop you winning a new job.

It sounds harsh and heartless to say it, but a new employer will not want to employ a bitter or self-pitying individual. They won't want to take on someone who appears not to respect his last employer, who holds a grudge against senior management and doesn't appreciate the realities of business economics. I am not saying this description applies to you, but if you're not careful that's exactly how you'll come across in a job interview.

'The most common negative feelings people report at the time of the redundancy are feeling upset, angry, stressed, bitter, betrayed and rejected. Many also feel shocked and anxious. The most common positive feelings are of being relieved and being free.'
REDUNDANCY TRANSFORMATIONS STUDY, ALTERNATIVE FUTURES, 2009

So make the conscious and explicit decision now – today – to be a bigger and better person than this. Leave bitterness behind.

Jane Francis did. She'd only just returned from maternity leave after the birth of her first child when the insurance company she worked for made massive job cuts. The department she worked in was reduced overnight from almost sixty people to fewer than twenty.

Jane recalls: 'At the time I was boiling over with anger. I was absolutely livid. It wasn't just that they were making cuts – it was also that they'd cut the whole department in half, those they wanted to keep and the rest, and they'd put me in the wrong half! I couldn't believe it!'

But time has been a healer for Jane. 'When I look back on it now, I regret how long I stayed angry and bitter about what had happened. I'd advise anyone in that situation now to find a way to offload it, release all that emotion, and move on.' Your emotional reaction can sometimes stop you from accessing help. 'I remember I very nearly turned down the chance to visit a Redundancy Counsellor, simply because it was being suggested by the company. That would have been a mistake. I'd say to anyone that if you're offered outside help, for goodness' sake take it! If you're not offered it you should push for it. It really helps to talk to someone who is independent, who is outside the company and has advised people in this situation before. It will help you get over your bitterness and plan a way forward.'

Leave bitterness behind. It's so easy to say, but very hard to do. So try this approach. Take a pad of paper and write down all your angry and bitter feelings about your redundancy. Put each feeling on a different page. Let rip! Say exactly what you really feel! Put all of your emotions into it. Don't mince words.

After you've done this task and filled the pad with all your most negative thoughts, have a break. Drink a cup of tea or take a walk. On your return take up these sheets of paper, one at a time and quite slowly, quite deliberately tear them up. Destroy them! Scrunch them into a ball and throw them into your bin. One at a time, watch them go. You've chosen to ditch these attitudes, to bury all of this anger, to destroy all of these resentments. Resolve that this is the last you and anyone else will see of them!

In their place you will have to practise a few phrases that you can identify with. These are phrases you will use every time your redundancy is mentioned. Whether you are speaking to your partner, your friends, acquaintances or are in a job interview, these new phrases are going to describe what you feel now, and how you are dealing with the situation. Here are some examples of phrases you might use, though you need to discover your own words that you feel comfortable with:

- 'I felt upset at the time but I've moved on now.'
- 'It's been hard but I've actually learned a lot about myself as a result.'
- 'It's been a big challenge, but I'm only looking forwards now with a new focus.'

- 'I've been thinking about changing career direction for some time now. It's taken this to spur me into doing it. I know now where I want to be in future.'
- 'If I'm honest with myself I really wasn't enjoying my last job and was starting to think about a change. Now I'm looking forward to finding a new job that I can give my all to.'

Find the right words for you. With the right attitude, shorn of all bitterness and focused on the future, you can begin to move on. Go to it!

11 ASK YOURSELF THE RIGHT QUESTIONS

At this precise moment you are probably seeking a lot of answers. But first you need to ask yourself the right questions!

Successful people don't know all the answers. No one does. A sense of humility in this area is appropriate. But one thing that successful people have in common is that they ask themselves the right questions.

The question you may, quite naturally, be asking yourself right now is 'How do I find another job like my last one?' But as many of the ideas and individual case studies in this book illustrate, the right move for you may not be to find another job – at least, not now and not in exactly the same sector or role as before. Most people who experi-

'We are not the creatures of circumstance, we are the creators of circumstance.'
BENJAMIN DISRAELI

ence redundancy do not move back into the same role as before. New opportunities beckon: you might retrain for a new career, launch your own business or downshift to a different life.

To find the right answers, you first need to find the right questions.

The questions you might ask yourself could be:

- Who can help me right now?
- What is the right job for me to do at this stage in my career?
- What work could I do that would really make me happy?
- What jobs am I equipped to do?
- How else can I earn as much money as I did in my last job?

- What would I choose to do if money wasn't the object?
- How much money do I really need to earn?
- Where do I really want to be in ten years' time?
- What jobs are going to be in demand during a downturn that I would be good at?

These are my questions, not yours. They are just there to illustrate some of the different questions you might ask.

Asking yourself the right questions is the first step towards reaching the right answers.

For my own part, when I set up my own business after redundancy, I asked myself the question 'What have I really got to lose if I start my own business and fail?' I realised the answer was that it wouldn't be a problem to me, I could always go back to my other career. So I decided to go for it and review the situation after twelve months. I discovered in that time that I could be successful running my own business. I also discovered that I loved it. Now I wouldn't go back to working in the corporate world.

So start by making a list of your own questions. Discuss them with the people you trust: your partner, friends and family. Discuss them with your coach or careers adviser.

Which questions *feel right* to you?

Now for the second difficult task. Don't answer these questions straight away. Whatever you do, don't rush to judgement. Give the questions time to take hold in your mind. Sleep on them.

Gradually, over the coming days and weeks, the correct answers will start to come to you. Be patient.

12 RETRAIN FOR A NEW CAREER

The time when a person had one job throughout their entire working life has passed. Perhaps the time when a person has only one career is passing too.

It may well be time for you to embrace a new career. Why not use this opportunity to retrain?

When you think about it, it's obvious isn't it? When you first started out there were hundreds of possible jobs you could have done. Now you know much more than you did then. The number of possible jobs you might do has increased, not decreased. It is only your beliefs about yourself that are stopping you.

'Around one person in ten retrains for a new career following redundancy.'
REDUNDANCY TRANSFORMATIONS STUDY, ALTERNATIVE FUTURES, 2009

Are you guilty of pigeonholing yourself? You have a wide variety of skills. Some were being used to the full in your last job, others partially or not at all. Some of your skills are dormant. Some skills may have begun to wither on the vine, from lack of use, but might be reawakened by retraining. You have other talents where the addition of some up-to-date knowledge could make a big difference!

One option open to you is to retrain, to shift your career decisively in a different direction. If you look around, you may be surprised to find how much financial help is available for certain types of retraining. You may also find some free or inexpensive courses (for example in basic computing skills or office skills) on offer that can help with your all-round employability. The Careers Advice Service, funded by the government, offers free careers advice and counselling. It may be helpful in identifying career directions and training courses that are suitable for you. Career Development Loans (currently of between £300 and £8000) are interest-free during the retraining period and can be obtained for a wide variety of approved retraining courses. They may also cover other course costs and some living expenses during the period of retraining. You can find information about these loans from Directgov.

'In difficult market conditions, redefining yourself is difficult. Employers can easily find square pegs to fit in square holes. If you are trying to redefine yourself, you may need to invest substantially in retraining and be prepared to take a stepping stone approach to your new career'.

KATE FARRINGTON, PRINCIPAL CAREER CONSULTANT, PENNA

Private organisations, including leading outplacement consultancies such as Penna, can also provide coaching and careers advice help to individuals. Although employers most commonly pay for outplacement support, private individuals can sometimes access support services directly. Some people choose to pay for this support out of their redundancy payment as an investment in their future.

Career transition services offered by private companies include services such as psychometric testing (to understand your personality type) and career anchoring (to establish what kinds of jobs and role you are suited to). You can also access personal coaching, interview skills training, executive job search and recruitment consultancy through this kind of company. People whose lives have been transformed in a positive way following redundancy are more likely to have used career transition or outplacement support.

RETRAINING FOR A NEW CAREER – A CASE STUDY

After graduating in chemistry, Robert took a job as a Research Scientist with an international chemicals company. He worked initially in the UK for a time and then was reassigned to a technical management role in Spain. However, the chemicals plant in Barcelona was sold while he was based there. Robert was made redundant and returned to the UK in 1990 to seek work.

Robert decided to give his career a boost by taking an MBA at the Cranfield School of Management. This was a significant investment but he felt confident it would lead to him finding a good job afterwards. 'I had seen another colleague with an MBA progressing really rapidly in his career and believed it would do the same for mine. I thought with an MBA I would find a good job quite easily – unfortunately, that didn't prove to be the case.' The British economy was in some difficulty in 1991 and he had a year of frustration immediately after gaining his MBA. He carried out various temporary jobs during this time. Robert realised that once again he needed to try something different: 'I decided to look closely at the types of job which were in demand and to think about retraining for those areas.'

There were a few teachers in Robert's extended family. His brother-in-law invited Robert to come down and stay for a week with the Science Department at his public school. Whilst Robert was there he was able to watch various teachers in action. 'I watched the science teachers taking lessons and thought to myself "I could do that!" I also knew there was a real shortage of science teachers in the UK at that time, which encouraged me to think this would be the right move for me.'

So Robert took a Career Development Loan and retrained again. He also considered personal coaching as he knew he didn't always come across as well at interviews as he should. After gaining his PGCE (Post Graduate Certificate of Education) he quickly found a job as a science teacher at a leading boys' school, where he progressed rapidly to become Head of Science.

The main lessons Robert learned were: 'Never give up. Consider retraining for something you'll be good at, and which is in demand. Also be brave enough to accept if you've taken a wrong turning. With hindsight, taking an MBA proved to be the wrong move for me. Don't lose sleep over it, just admit it and move on.'

13 INCREASE YOUR SKILL SET

Make yourself more employable. Invest some time (and perhaps a little money) to increase your skill set. Keep your knowledge up-to-date. The fact that you've made a big effort to do this will impress an employer.

The chances are that your next job is *not* going to be the same as the job that you've just left. It's a simple fact of life: the future is going to look different for you. You might not yet have the full complement of skills yet to take you into your next job or to run your own business successfully.

So you need to think hard about increasing your skill set in whatever ways you can. Look around for opportunities for free or fully funded training. For instance, if you're considering starting up your own business, you may find a variety of free training seminars arranged by organisations such as Business Link and your bank.

Local evening classes can be an excellent and low-cost way of topping up your skills. Perhaps a foreign language or two would be helpful and look good on your CV? Maybe you need to top up your IT skills? Or perhaps some improvement in your presentation skills or assertiveness would make all the difference in your next job?

If you feel you need extensive training to prepare you for a new career, a longer course may be appropriate. You might consider investing some of your redundancy money in some major retraining. Alternatively, consider taking out a Career Development Loan. Career Development Loans of up to £8000 are available for a wide variety of approved retraining courses. Find information about these loans from Directgov or through banks such as Royal Bank of Scotland, Barclays or the Co-operative Bank.

There are a variety of low-cost ways of increasing your skill set and making yourself more employable. For instance, if you network effectively, you will soon create a professional network of individuals who can support you – and you can support – through the months ahead. Try running a 'training exchange' with them. Here you offer to train someone else in a subject you know about if they will train you in return on their specialist subject. Perhaps someone who is experienced in using PowerPoint or Excel software might arrange to train someone who has excellent presentation skills and be trained on how to become a better presenter in return. This kind of exchange with professional contacts can apply to more than just training – you will find a professional network will benefit you in lots of ways.

We age and decline or we age and grow – make sure you do the latter!

If you want to break into a new area consider this thought: why not try to 'shadow' a person who works in that field? Say that you want to break into PR and your friend's sister works in that field. Ask if you can shadow her for a day or two to understand what the job involves. You should offer to do this on an unpaid basis, of course. If there's an opportunity to move beyond shadowing and help actively in some way, then seize it! For instance, you might offer to take notes for her during meetings and type them up afterwards.

Voluntary work can be a way of keeping your skills up to date. Perhaps you've been out of the office environment for a while and could volunteer to help in the Head Office of a charity? The mere fact of being immersed in an office again will help refresh your skills.

Public libraries provide a practical, free way of training yourself. If you need to understand an industry before you apply for a job there, you can carry out research at a library for free. If you want to begin to train yourself in a new career – sales or marketing, teaching or coaching, finance or consultancy, publishing or PR, computing or catering – you can do worse than begin by reading some books on the subject. If you do decide to train yourself, do it properly. Make detailed notes as you go through the book. Type these notes up later. Talk them through with someone else. By the time you have done this, the points will have passed through your head at least three times. Read, write and recall! You will find you remember the points you have learned and can talk about them when questioned. So when you go for that job interview, you can begin to demonstrate a grasp of the subject as a result of your own self-study. You can impress an employer with your initiative. You may even be able to quote from leading industry figures.

Become a better person during your 'redundancy break'. Make a real effort to expand your knowledge and improve your skills over this time. Develop your understanding of new careers and professions.

14 TAKE VOLUNTARY WORK

Voluntary work is not just a way of keeping your mind and body active, or an opportunity to do some good in this world and make yourself feel better. It can also, sometimes, lead you to make important new connections and even into a new career.

If you find yourself with time on your hands following your redundancy, there are some very simple *dos* and *don'ts* to observe. Observing them, however, requires a strong degree of self-discipline:

- Don't oversleep: long lie-ins will leave you feeling lethargic and dispirited.
- Do keep active.
- Don't waste your days watching daytime TV.
- Do get out and meet people.
- Don't be self-critical.
- Do give yourself praise where it is due.

Voluntary work is a good way to make sure you tick off some of the *dos* on your list and avoid some of the *don'ts*. It does many things for you all at once: it feeds your self-esteem, it keeps you active and it gets

> *'The best way to cheer yourself up is to cheer somebody else up.'*
>
> MARK TWAIN

you out into the world where you can make new contacts. If you are able to use your professional skill – if you're an IT professional and you offer to help a local charity to develop the IT skills of their office staff, for example – then you can keep your experience up to date. You can use the act of volunteering to keep your hand in. Perhaps you can even spot an opportunity to volunteer for something that will expand your skill set?

Voluntary work might show you a path into a new career. After all, there is more to life than making money. You may find working in the not-for-profit sector sparks something off in you that you really hadn't expected. You may suddenly realise you'd like to work in this sector and discover exactly how you might make a worthwhile contribution. Even if it doesn't set off a desire to work in the sector, you will be making contacts through your voluntary work. Any one of these contacts could be a good networking contact for you. With networking it is not necessarily whether the person you are talking to can help you, but whether they know someone who can help you. All networking contacts can be promising contacts.

VOLUNTEERING – A CASE STUDY

Here's the story of how Tony went from a commercial career to be a project co-ordinator for a major national charity.

Tony had been working as a customer support manager in the aerospace industry. After twenty-five years with his employer, he found himself being made redundant when the company was involved in a merger and his role was duplicated in the other organisation. It wasn't a good time to be looking for another job in this sector. 'So many other people in the industry were in exactly the same position as me,' he explains. He spent eight months looking for jobs and was having no luck whatsoever. 'At the time I was only getting around 20% of my letters answered. I was starting to feel quite despondent when a chance occurrence changed my life. A friend of mine had recently lost her husband. She'd been invited (there was an announcement at her church) to go along to a Volunteers Day that was being held by a charity. The charity wanted to talk to people who might be persuaded to volunteer. They wanted to talk to them over tea and biscuits, and show them different ways they might help. My friend didn't want to go on her own. She knew I'd do anything for a cup of tea and a biscuit, so she asked me if I'd go along with her.'

Tony's friend never did find any voluntary work with the charity that she could fit in with her other commitments, but Tony did. 'A couple of days later, I was phoned up by the Volunteers Co-ordinator for the charity, to see if I could help with some administrative work in the Membership Department. At first I was working as a volunteer on one afternoon a week, though it quickly went up to two afternoons. Just doing basic admin really – answering letters, taking phone calls, that sort of thing. After about six months a contract job came up with the charity to do administrative work on a paid basis. They asked me if I'd like to do it. The contract was then extended to twelve months.'

After a brief break back in the commercial world, Tony is now back working in a full-time role with the same charity as a project co-ordinator in the Youth and Education Department. He says this of the shift which has taken place in his working life. 'I'm happier than I was at the end of my aerospace career, for sure. It's not a rat race here! I work with a lovely bunch of people and I enjoy going to work each day. I have a much better work-life balance than I had previously.'

Could the act of volunteering help your life take a new direction?

15 FULFIL A LIFELONG AMBITION

You've been handed a career break. This may not be the way you had planned it, but you've now got the opportunity to use the time to do something special. Only you will know what that 'something special' is going to be. What have you always dreamed of doing?

The vast majority of us dream of a new and different life. And at any one time, one in three of us is dreaming of quitting our job.

Well, you've left your former employer – perhaps not as you planned – and now you can create a new and different life for yourself.

What's your lifelong ambition? Travelling the world, running in a marathon, doing a long-distance walk, writing a book, climbing a mountain, learning a musical instrument, acting in a play, having your works of art formally exhibited – or something else?

We all have different ambitions. They may be challenging aspirations but they say a lot about what we believe our lives are for. If you were now at the end of your life, looking back, what is it that you would regret never having made time for? Perhaps now is the time to do it!

Probably the most important message we've received from participants in the Redundancy Transformations Study (a survey looking at the experiences of those who've experienced redundancy and then transformed their lives) is this: stay positive. Keep going, don't stop, and set yourself a target and a time limit. If you decide to use this time to fulfil a lifelong ambition, you will inevitably stay positive. It's what you've always wanted to do! You'll stay active, throwing yourself into the challenge of making it happen. You'll feel positive about yourself and will have achieved something you always hoped you would do.

Here's what Alan, one of the respondents on the Redundancy Transformations Study, had to say: 'When I was made redundant I was 49 years old, comfortably off, with no ties. So I took myself off and rode my motorcycle round the world. I did more and saw more in three years than some people would in several lifetimes. Nobody can ever take any of that away from me! I learned a huge amount about the world, people, and myself.'

If after this kind of experience you come to seek a job, you will have something that sets you apart at a job interview. You will be able to talk about achieving something that demonstrates your drive and ambition, and shows your planning abilities and your commitment to achieving your life goals.

'During this period, after being made redundant, we often advise candidates to strive to achieve something else in their lives apart from getting a new job. Whether it is learning a new language, running a marathon, or some other achievement – it doesn't really matter. It gives the individual a boost, a new success in their lives – and something else to talk about in job interviews!'

KATE FARRINGTON, PRINCIPAL CAREER CONSULTANT, PENNA

If you tell your interviewer that your next goal now is to get this job, that you're completely committed to this industry and this particular role, are they likely to doubt you?

16 RECHARGE YOUR BATTERIES

The torch won't work if the battery is flat. You need to shine at a job interview. You need to be enthusiastic, passionate, fully charged! Take some time out to recharge your batteries – but don't take too long.

If you are still in the immediate aftermath of redundancy, this chapter is for you.

Make a deliberate decision to recharge your batteries before you take any major actions to get your next job and take any far-reaching decisions. You have to get over the shock first. Treat yourself gently for a short while. Stay calm. Take a week or two off to begin considering your options and mulling over your next move.

By taking time off, I don't mean do nothing – I mean give yourself a break. If you love sport then play tennis, badminton, football or squash, or go swimming or hiking. If you love travel, try to get away for a week or at least a long weekend. If you love gardening, throw yourself into that and give your mind time to begin to digest what has happened to you.

During this brief period – and it is important to keep it brief (no more than a few weeks, because passivity is not about to be the new pattern for your life) – you are doing three things:

- Giving your mind time to adjust to the new realities.
- Beginning to think about your career options.
- Avoiding any premature actions that will begin to take you down the wrong path for you at this pivotal moment.

Give your mind time to adjust to the new realities and your body time to recharge its batteries. Do this for a short time and then put all your energies into building your new life.

Remember the six-word formula for success: 'Think things through then follow through'. That's what you need to do right now, but you will need fully charged batteries to give you the power to follow through.

While recharging your batteries, make conscious decisions that will help to take stress out of your life. Set aside time for reading, meditation or for a short walk. If you have a dog that needs exercise you are especially fortunate, because dogs are excellent stress-busters.

Seek out the sunshine. If you find the sun is shining for half an hour during the day, get out in it.

For all the negatives that sometimes come from redundancy, there is one single, massive positive: you are free.

Free to choose a new career if you want to.

Free to choose to work on a different basis in future – for instance, working part-time to give yourself a better work-life balance.

Free to work in future from a location that suits you – for instance, as a freelancer working from home.

Free to fulfil your lifelong ambitions.

Free to start your own business if you would like to be your own boss.

Take a moment to think of all of the positives that could flow from your new-found freedom. Feel the lightness of spirit this thought provokes. With your batteries fully charged you can take your life in any direction you want from here. The future is up to you!

17 CARRY OUT A SKILLS AUDIT ON YOURSELF

A skills audit may help you. It helps you appreciate the variety of jobs you are capable of fulfilling. It breaks open any rigid definition of your potential that may be holding you back. It fuels your self-esteem by reminding you of all the talents you have.

You are a multi-talented individual. Don't deny it: we all are. Here in the UK, we are masters of modesty. Given a chance, we will be self-effacing. If people pay us a compliment, we are most likely to deny it.

Have we ever stopped to think how foolish that makes the person offering the compliment feel? So perhaps it is time for us to do something different and do it openly, honestly and thoroughly. It's time for us to admit to ourselves the wide range of skills and talents that we have.

To make sure you do this thoroughly, set aside a whole day for this task. If you take this exercise seriously it will certainly help you.

Get a sheet of paper and head it with the words 'Skills audit'. You need two columns – one for your core skills (the things you are particularly good at) and one for all the other skills you possess (some of which you might need to brush up on). Please don't edit your list mentally in advance: put down absolutely every skill you believe you have in one or other of these two columns.

Start by going back in time to your schooldays. Think of all the things you learned at school and throughout your academic life. What subjects were you naturally good at? What skills did you emerge from school

We each tend to underestimate the range of skills we possess and overestimate the skills of others. Typically, many of our skills are dormant – by reawakening and updating them we can make ourselves more employable.

with? You might find already you can enter on your sheet some or all of the following: numeracy, literacy, interpersonal communications and foreign language skills. Don't stop there! Think hard and make your list as long as possible.

Now go on to your personal life and itemise all the skills your hobbies, interests and enthusiasms have brought you. You might now be able to add skills such as driving, car mechanics, computer skills, gardening, painting and decorating, art, childcare, planning and organisation, and so on to the list.

Move onto the jobs you have held. Take each one in turn. For each job, go through all of the skills you needed to do that job. What sort of skills would an employer now be asking for if they wanted to fill that kind of vacancy? Write them down, all of them. You must have had this skill, at least to some extent, to have worked successfully in that role. If the job involved organisation skills, management skills, team leadership, diplomacy, assertiveness, negotiation skills, salesmanship, problem-solving, budgeting skills or IT skills, then write them down and be as specific as you can. Remember to include skills you learned at training courses and any on-the-job training that you were given.

When you believe you have finished your skills audit, try asking some people who know you well (such as close friends or former colleagues) what they think your main skills are. Phrase your question in a general way and be welcoming and accepting of whatever they say. Don't argue with them. If they believe you are good at something, pay them the respect that's due and thank them for holding that positive view of you. Don't dismiss what they say. If you hadn't got the skill they have mentioned on your list already, then add it to the list.

Now for the most important and exciting part. By grouping skills together in different ways, you can see that your 'skill set', this collection of skills, equips you to perform a range of different jobs. You are not actually fixed to one particular role, industry or career. You are a flexible individual, capable of working in a variety of roles.

Try writing down each skill onto a separate card. You can modify a pack of playing cards for this. Then group your skills together in different ways and ask yourself 'If I was using these (three, four or five) skills together, what jobs could I do?'

Here's a simplified example. Let's suppose that Martin was formerly a Business Analyst. His skills audit revealed skills such as interviewing skills, presentation skills, analysis skills, numeracy, organisation skills and time management. Comments from Martin's partner suggested she admired him particularly because he's a self-starter with a lot of drive who plans things and makes things happen on his own initiative. She also thought he was very articulate and persuasive whenever he was putting a point across. By grouping his skills together in different ways, Martin might realise he was actually suited to several different careers:

Nothing holds us back so much as our own fixed view of ourselves.

- Sales (interviewing skills + presentation skills + time-management skills + drive + persuasiveness).
- Market research (interviewing skills + numeracy + analysis skills + presentation skills).
- Maths teacher (presentation skills + numeracy + organisation skills + time management).

So what are your main skills? What else might you do with them?

18 REDRAFT YOUR CV

Your CV is a document to sell you. It is there to persuade an employer to interview you. That's all. If you haven't updated it recently, it's time for a redraft!

It may have been some time since you were last looking for a job. The world has moved on. You need to make sure your CV is fully up to date, not just in terms of its content but in terms of its whole look and feel.

Once CVs were simply lists of job descriptions and dates. Now they tend to focus on achievements and highlight the difference a person has made to the organisations they've worked for.

Preparing your CV should not be a casual, low-energy exercise. You need to put your all into it. You want all that you are and can offer an employer to emerge from reading it. The target is to write a short CV: just two pages of A4 paper is the maximum advisable length. To write a short document, you generally need to write a longer one first and then edit it carefully. It's proof of the old adage that the shorter the document is, the longer it actually takes to write! While some people do produce effective CVs covering just a single page, or as many as three pages, the two-page CV has become widely accepted CV etiquette. Don't depart from this format unless you have a very strong reason.

Your CV needs to be concise and easy to read. It needs to be punchy and have impact. Employers spend very little time studying each CV they receive – frequently under a minute – so you need your strong points to jump out of the page at them. For this reason, 'less is more' – the more words you write, the greater the chance that the employer will overlook the points you wanted to communicate.

Here are the headings for a standard CV:

- Contact details
- Summary (or Profile)
- Educational and professional qualifications
- Experience (including career highlights/main achievements)
- Referees.

As part of your contact details you should give your name and home address, and also a phone number that you can be contacted on for a confidential conversation. You may wish to include a mobile number as well here. It's not generally a good idea to give the telephone number of your current employer.

'Many employers in our experience will spend under a minute looking over a CV, so it is crucial to make yours as succinct and impactful as possible,'

KATE FARRINGTON, PRINCIPAL CAREER CONSULTANT, PENNA

The *Summary* or *Profile* is increasingly important. Many CVs now feature a short summary statement, often in a box to give it greater impact, that allows the reader to see at a glance the key details of the applicant. Here are some examples of Profile statements:

- 'Part-qualified Accountant with twelve years' experience in the retail sector and excellent inter-personal skills.'
- 'Experienced and dynamic NPD Director with track record of bringing successful new insurance products to market.'
- 'Fully qualified, experienced Catering Manager with proven team management and motivational skills.'

Try for a moment to summarise yourself and your career experience in twenty words or less. You need to find the best, most powerful encapsulation of your career experience and character. This profile statement is the equivalent of a personal advert. It needs to persuade someone who doesn't know you to take a chance on you and agree to meet up! Some jobseekers find it helpful to use different versions of their CVs, each employing slightly different profile statements and CV content, when applying for different jobs. This allows them to match the areas they emphasise to the areas that each employer is particularly asking for. But if you do this, be careful to remember which version of the CV you've used on which occasions. Your computer may soon store several different CVs – don't mix them up!

In the section on *Educational and professional qualifications*, you can be pragmatic in how briefly you describe some qualifications. If you have a degree or post-graduate qualifications, the subjects and grades for your O levels are no longer terribly relevant. Saying simply, for instance, 'Eight O levels' will suffice.

The *Experience* section of your CV is where you list your previous jobs, employers and dates, beginning with the most recent and working backwards. When mentioning employment dates (From/To) it is normally sufficient simply to mention the years, not the months. You don't need to go into as much detail for temporary or short-term employment as you do for an employer where you worked for ten years! Make sure you highlight your main career achievements in this section. What difference have you made?

When replying directly to job ads, matching your experience and the employer's requirements is a good idea. It shows at a glance that you 'tick all the boxes' and should be invited for interview. For instance, if you show two columns in your covering letter as in the example below, you demonstrate that you meet the employer's requirements:

You are asking for:	I offer:
Minimum of three years' experience in logistics	Five years' logistics management experience
Graduate-calibre individual	Degree in Business Studies
Ability to lead a small team	Experience of managing a department of seven people

19 REGISTER WITH RECRUITMENT CONSULTANTS

You can find a new job by answering job ads directly, through recruitment consultants or executive search agencies, and via your own networking contacts.

It is a sensible move to register with at least one recruitment consultant once you know what kind of job you are looking for.

Registering with one recruitment consultant (or several) is one of the first actions most people take after losing their job. In practice, it can be that this action 'jumps the gun', leading people rapidly into the decision to seek another job just like their last one.

The best time to register with recruitment consultants is *after* you've decided what you want to do next. This could mean that the right time to register is not immediately after being made redundant, but a few weeks later. If the recruitment consultants are to match you to the right job opportunities, you need to be clear with them what career direction you are committed to. If you fail to say this clearly at interview, you may find that the only jobs that are mentioned to you are those that are very similar to your last role.

You will only escape being typecast by being absolutely clear about your future intentions and what kinds of roles you will and won't consider. You do need to be realistic: some jobs you might like to do will require extensive retraining before you will ever be considered. Some roles require significant prior experience as an entry point. You may need to use a 'stepping stone' approach, taking more junior roles until you can establish a track record. Sometimes the only way round a brick wall is to take one step back, two steps to the side and then walk round it!

There are several different kinds of recruitment consultants you might consider approaching:

- *Executive search consultants* (or 'head-hunters') deal with the most senior level appointments, typically roles at board level and above.
- *Specialist recruitment consultants* focus on specific industries or specific types of job. You will discover the main recruitment consultants covering your industry from talking to your peers or from reading the trade magazines covering your industry or profession.
- *General recruitment consultants* cover all kinds of jobs and every kind of industry. They may also cover a range of part-time and temporary work.
- *Online recruitment agencies* offer a less personalised service but may help to ensure that your CV reaches a wide audience.

When you are invited for interview with a recruitment consultancy, you should prepare for that interview as thoroughly and professionally as you would an interview with an employer. Dress in the same way you would for an interview with an employer. The interview is likely, in effect, to be your first interview for several different potential employers: all the employers who are using that recruitment consultancy to fill their vacancies. So this interview may be more important in opening up your job prospects than any single employer interview.

Many senior jobs are not advertised directly. It is sensible to register with recruitment consultants and network actively to supplement advertised vacancies.

This is one reason why isn't always a good idea to register with every recruitment consultancy you can think of, all at once. If you see all these agencies in the fortnight immediately after you are made redundant, for instance, you will give them all exactly the same steer on your future career direction. Yet your views on your future career may evolve over the months immediately following your redundancy. Your interview skills may also increase over the months following your redundancy as you become more practised at interviews. You may not cut as impressive a figure when you are still reeling from the shock of the redundancy.

Having been interviewed by a recruitment consultancy, put some effort into maintaining contact with them. Phone your consultant to enquire about progress and begin to build a relationship. Keep yourself at the front of his mind. Keep your consultant updated on any changes in your own situation – for example, if you've decided, on reflection, that you'd now consider relocating to other parts of the country or if you have just completed some training that widens the scope of jobs you can be considered for.

Don't put all your eggs in one basket. Registering with a recruitment consultant is not a reason to just switch off and sit back. You will almost certainly wish to pursue other activities at the same time as this: things you can do yourself, including networking and replying to job advertisements that employers have placed directly.

Keep calm, don't panic. Register with only one or two carefully selected recruitment consultancies in the first instance, keeping the others in reserve for later. Keep some of your powder dry. Your interview technique will improve over time and your future plans will become firmer.

20 MARKET YOURSELF ONLINE

Things will start to happen for you if you make the right connections. The Internet has provided new ways for you to make those connections. Online marketing works for companies and products – it can also work for you.

Twenty years ago there was only one way to make a job application: paper and pen, filling in a detailed application form and then posting it off. Now you are quite likely to complete an online application form.

If you email your CV to someone who already knows you and who you have spoken to recently, you will have increased your chances of it being considered.

Twenty years ago, there was only one way you'd have got your CV to an employer. You would have had it painstakingly typed up, then photocopied, and posted it with a covering letter to the employer. Now you can use the power of the Internet to put your CV in front of many potential employers, through online recruitment agencies and job websites.

Make a point of spending an hour Googling to identify all the online recruitment websites that might help you. Make sure you are registered with the most important websites, providing them with up-to-date profile and CV information. Use these websites to search for jobs and ensure your CV reaches the widest possible audience.

Speculative applications can be sent to companies by email. However, if you send your CV to someone who already knows you – who you have spoken to recently – you will have increased your chances of it being considered. Similarly if, you can get someone who knows the recipient to forward your CV, you will have increased your chances. This is particularly the case if they forward it saying 'This is the CV of someone I've met and been impressed with, who I think might be useful for you to see.'

Twenty years ago, there were only a few ways you'd have networked with friends: face-to-face and by phone. Now you can text and email. Now you can use social networking websites like Facebook to keep in touch. Perhaps even more importantly when it comes to jobseeking, there are business networking websites like LinkedIn, which you can use to reconnect with working colleagues from your previous workplaces.

We live in an online world. Online marketing can help you too!

You can use online facilities like Yahoo Groups to form a club – your own redundancy support group, for instance. You might like to give it a more interesting name, but this is what it is! Use Yahoo Groups to send messages between yourselves, give tips and recommend useful websites to one another. Post meeting dates and venues online so that everyone knows where to meet and when.

Maintain email contact with as many people as possible. Be open with them about your current situation. Let them see how energised you are by the quest to find a new job. Crucially, though – even if you are technically minded or particularly IT-literate – don't give priority to online contact above face-to-face meetings. Any salesman will confirm this: nothing works better than meeting people. However, online and offline actions can certainly complement each other.

Here's an example of how online and offline actions can work together. You might email an old friend or former colleague and suggest meeting up to catch up on all their news. You're not being selfish or false about this: you genuinely like them and want to hear about them. You meet them over lunch or a coffee – you should offer to pay the bill – and mention that you are in career transition and that you're now looking for a job in a particular role. They mention in return that they know someone who used to work in that kind of role. They offer to put you in touch so you can find out more about what the job involves. They also mention what's going on in their life and you find there's something you can do to help them too. Afterwards, you exchange further emails, do these little favours for one another and arrange to meet again. A few days later you meet their friend, who turns out to now be retired but to still have good contacts with his former employer. He offers to email your CV on to one of his contacts at that employer, if you will email him a copy. Voilà! You've created a job opportunity out of thin air.

21 PRACTISE YOUR ELEVATOR SPEECH

You need to learn how to sell yourself succinctly, memorably and persuasively, at a networking gathering, in a phone call to a prospective employer or at a job interview.

First impressions are the most powerful impressions of all. You need to find the right words to put yourself across to someone else in thirty seconds or less.

'So what's your line of work?' is the innocuous question at a dinner party. Or it might be: 'What do you do for a living?' The answer you give might light up their eyes or cause you and them to squirm with embarrassment. The best answer will set their interest alight and make them want to find out more about you. The best answer will immediately cause them to empathise with you: it will put them on your side.

It's the same at networking gatherings. You have only a short time to make an impression. You need to make every word count in your favour, and avoid saying anything that will make the person who has asked the question regret asking it. Remember that your body language and tone of voice is also going to be at least as important as the words you use. You generally need to strive to be friendly, confident, warm and outgoing. And it is the same in job interviews, too – prospective employers will form an opinion of you within the first five minutes of any interview. That's why preparing an elevator speech (or elevator pitch) is so important.

The term 'elevator speech' comes from the idea that a junior employee might, by chance, share the same lift as the Chief Executive. Imagine that the lift is travelling from the ground floor to the tenth floor. They are the only two people in the lift. The Chief Executive looks at the junior employee and asks 'So what do you do?' What do they say in reply? They have thirty short seconds at most before the lift arrives at its destination. Thirty seconds to make an impression on the most powerful person in the company. Whatever those words are, they need to be accurate and impactful.

The nature of a good elevator speech is punchy, snappy and upbeat. A distillation of who you are, condensed and served up in a bottle.

Why should I do this, you might be thinking? It'll make me sound arrogant, it'll sound false and prepared. No one will like to hear me blowing my own trumpet! Well, that's only going to be the case if the elevator speech *you* prepare sounds arrogant and false. It needs to be authentic, it needs to be accurate – it needs to reflect *you*.

Having prepared an elevator speech, you may find you never use it – not word for word, anyway. The things you say on each occasion are natural outflowings, using some of the elevator speech phrases. But by preparing an elevator speech, and practising it in private, you will find the right words come to you more readily whenever you're asked this kind of question. Having a prepared elevator speech, a ready answer up your sleeve to the obvious first question, gives you immense confidence when you're breaking the ice with someone new. Whether you ever use your elevator speech in its entirety or not is up to you. But prepare it and practise it.

> *The nature of a good elevator speech is punchy, snappy and upbeat. A distillation of who you are, condensed and served up in a bottle.*

Clearly you have one issue you need to address. How do you refer to your recent employment and your current situation? Do you mention you have just been made redundant? How much you say is up to you, and will probably vary a little depending on the setting. The following possible elevator speeches might help. Note that they are all five sentences or less in length. They need to be short and quick to deliver.

- 'I'm Martha. I'm at a career transition point at the moment. I've been working in a number of healthcare jobs, most recently as a contract nurse in a private hospital, but I'm looking in future to specialise in long-term nursing care for the elderly. I think that's where the main needs are going to be in future.'

- 'My name is Alan. I've just left my job as a salesman for a top Japanese car manufacturer after ten years in the business. It's a really difficult time for the whole car industry right now! But I've always enjoyed selling high-ticket items to really affluent individuals – it's something I really enjoy. So I'm planning to use those niche sales skills in a new setting.'

- 'My name is Sonia. I've been working as a PA for fifteen years but the company I worked for has just been taken over. So I've gone freelance and have my own virtual PA business now. I'm looking to work with a mix of small and large companies, providing flexible administrative support when they need it.'

- 'Hi, I'm Peter. I'm a specialist in marketing copywriting. I've been working in marketing for over twenty years, most recently with a marketing consultancy which was taken over. So now I'm running my own copywriting business, helping companies with the wording of their sales brochures and website content.'

- 'I'm George, pleased to meet you. I've been working as a Local Government Planning Officer for most of my career but have decided it is time for a change. I'm looking to retrain as a Careers Adviser, as I've helped many internal colleagues over the years with career change decisions. I'm part-way through a specialist course which is going to equip me with all the skills I need.'

Having heard them, do you feel warmly disposed to the speaker? Do you feel intrigued and want to know more? Is a follow-up question on your lips? If so, the elevator speech has done its job!

Now it's time to prepare *your own* elevator speech. Go to it – and good luck!

22 RESEARCH OTHER CAREERS

You know you'd like to do something different – but what? Doing your homework on other career options is a sensible step to take right now.

It's a common dilemma. You've been made redundant from one job and feel it is time for a change in your life.

Perhaps your last job never really felt right for you. Or perhaps the industry you've been part of is not likely to be recruiting for some time, so you feel compelled to think afresh.

But what else can you do? What other careers are you equipped for? What other jobs might you be good at, if you had appropriate retraining? You need to start by taking a hard look at yourself: the things you enjoy doing and what you are good at. You also need to be candid with yourself about the things you don't enjoy doing and what you struggle with. This should begin to narrow down the search.

You also need to examine all the jobs you have carried out in your career until now. What aspects of the jobs appealed and what did you find difficult? Are there any obvious links between the jobs you did and job switches you might make right now? For instance, could the 'poacher turn gamekeeper' – could you switch from being a client to a supplier? Could you use your interpersonal skills in a different environment? Hopefully this kind of thinking will narrow the search down.

There are three main ways you can research new careers.

Firstly, take professional advice. If you received outplacement support, your outplacement company will probably have provided some career guidance coaching. If not, you might also choose to invest in help from private career counsellors. Alternatively the Careers Advice Service, funded by the government, offers simple and free careers advice. They may be helpful in identifying career directions and training courses for you to consider.

Secondly, do some detailed desk research. Harness the full power of the Internet and your nearest major public library. Look at published information by professional bodies and industry bodies to help you understand specific professions and roles. Locate articles that have been written about

Do your homework. Get yourself good information on other careers and you can begin to make the right choices.

that particular career. The Careers Advice Service website also allows you to take an online skills and interests assessment. This helpful website also allows you to look at hundreds of job profiles telling you what various jobs are like, what qualifications are needed and what pay and working hours you can expect. It can be a good start point.

Thirdly, use your networking contacts. Speak to everyone you meet about the jobs they do now and what they have done in the past. Discover what led them into their particular careers, whether they enjoy it, what the upsides and the downsides are. What qualifications did they need to get in? How did they find their jobs? Write up your notes on any job you're attracted to and then research that job further on the Internet. Go back to your contact and ask if they can introduce you to anyone else who does that job. The more people you can speak to in your chosen career, the better your understanding will be of what it's really like. You can clarify whether it seems like a career you would do well in. The more contacts you build up within your chosen career, the easier it will be to hear about entry-level job opportunities. Work the grapevine! You may even be able to use your network contacts as a way to secure some freelance work. This is a great way to develop your understanding of that career. If you have the opportunity to shadow someone in that career for a day, seize it! It will help you to learn and become an example for you to quote. This will be a way of demonstrating your enthusiasm for the role to a future employer.

The key to getting any job is having up-to-date and relevant skills. If your chosen career requires retraining, make sure you get the best training you can. Always remember, though, that employers will see many candidates with similar qualifications, so look for anything to improve your case that is 'over and above' the standard candidate offering. It will impress an employer if you have clearly used your initiative: you've researched that career, attended exhibitions and seminars at your own expense, and you've met with other people in different companies who do this job already.

In a difficult economic climate, it is particularly hard to move into a totally new career. However, by researching it thoroughly, you will put yourself in the best position to succeed.

23 SEEK CAREER GUIDANCE

You're standing at a crossroads now. The problem may be that you don't know which way to go from here. You don't even know which destinations can be reached by following the different directions.

If you feel uncertain, now is the time to seek professional career guidance. You don't know which way to turn, but you know you need advice.

But where can you go for career guidance in mid-career? If you're in the fortunate position of being provided with outplacement support by your former employer, as part of your redundancy package, then this will be the place to start.

Use any outplacement help that is offered to the full. Major outplacement companies like Penna will give extensive help with career-transition decisions by running workshops and one-to-one coaching sessions to help you find the right way forward. You will find that some outplacement companies also offer direct help to individuals who are prepared to pay for assistance if those individuals (as opposed to their employers) approach them directly.

According to many experts, the problem some people have is knowing where to start. A recent survey by One Life Live showed that more than a third of us would like to retrain for a new career but most of us don't know what career we'd like to retrain for! We know we want to take a new career direction, we're ready for a change, but don't really know what other careers would be appropriate. In the hands of a skilled careers adviser or coach, diagnostic tools like psychometric tests and Career Anchoring exercises can often help point the way forward.

Career Anchoring was developed by Edgar Schein, one of the founders of modern organisational psychology. The idea behind it is that each of us has a particular orientation towards work, approaching it with a certain set of priorities and values. These are our 'Career Anchors' – they are what motivate us, what drive us on. For you it might be all about challenge, or about dedication to a greater cause, while for others it might be about autonomy or technical competence.

Careers Advisers who use this technique sometimes discover that people have selected their current career for the wrong reasons. People find their responses in the workplace are incompatible with their true values. The result is that such people are unhappy and unproductive in their work. Do you feel that describes you when you were working for your last employer? If so, career coaching sessions can help you identify your true Career Anchors and perhaps point you in a new direction. Discover the real you: someone whose chosen career in future is in tune with your true priorities and values.

Don't make the mistake of defining your own capabilities too narrowly, and of simply seeking an identical role to the one you've lost.

'Career Anchoring worked for me' says Bob, one of the respondents on the Redundancy Transformations Study. 'It takes around thirty minutes' preparation and then an afternoon shut away with your Careers Coach. You need to go somewhere quiet where you can really focus. A good coach will ask tough questions and challenge you. It certainly forced me to think about what I wanted for the next one, five and ten years, so I could build a plan towards my future!'

If you aren't able to take up outplacement support and don't already have access to a Careers Adviser you can trust, then now is the time to seek one out! The Careers Advice Service is a publicly funded advice service.

You can have an initial free guidance session over the phone with one of their career coaches and take an online skills check. This may help you make the right first moves.

Careers Advisers often use psychometric tests to help them understand you as an individual. This enables them to give you better advice. Myers Briggs is one of the commonly used psychometric tests where you complete a questionnaire about yourself. The scores that emerge classify you according to four dimensions: Extrovert versus Introvert, Intuition versus Sensing, Thinking versus Feeling, Judgement versus Perception. Clearly the right role for an extrovert who intuitively feels their way through life's decisions and likes to take snap decisions is going to be different to that for an introverted thinker who always carries out detailed analysis and is cautious before acting.

The days of people having only one employer during their lifetimes have long passed. We are now witnessing the end of the time when people follow just a single career during their lifetime. What will be the second string to your bow?

If you are attracted to the idea of a career change but don't know what the options are, you need to find some professional careers advice. If you already know what career or job appeals, one of the best pieces of advice that can be given is to speak informally to as many people as possible who already do that job. Find out what the reality is, not the job description. What you imagine about that career may well be wide of the mark!

Somewhere within your contact network there is someone who knows someone who does that job. Appeal for help, track them down and try to speak to them. When you do, ask them what they love and hate about their job. What most surprised them about the job? Get them to explain what a typical day looks like. Enquire how they got their job and what advice they'd give to anyone who was looking to break into that career. If there is any possibility of shadowing them for a day or gaining unpaid job experience, then take it. This will give you a real insight into whether the job is genuinely one for you, before you commit yourself. It will also give you a contact within that role who might be willing to act as an informal mentor for you in future.

You are probably capable of much more than you think you are: capable of working in a wide number of different roles and of pursuing different careers. Take some advice from me: the first thing you need to do is to take some advice!

24 INVEST YOUR REDUNDANCY MONEY WISELY

The redundancy payment may be one of the largest sums of money you have ever received in your life. Use it wisely. Try to invest at least some of it.

Historically the average redundancy payment in the UK, according to a variety of different sources, has been around £10,000. It's a large sum of money.

Many people view their redundancy payment as money to tide them over until they find a new job. For most people, partly because that's how they see it, that's what it becomes. According to the Redundancy Transformations Study, a large majority of people spend their redundancy payment on day-to-day living expenses while they are looking for a new job – buying time and giving them some breathing space.

You might want to consider this thought, though. If you are able to *invest* this redundancy money to further one of your life's ambitions, you can turn this whole situation to your advantage. You can help make something positive happen in your life that would not otherwise have occurred. You might invest your redundancy money in retraining for a new career so

'We see many people who are faced with taking important financial decisions soon after their lives have been turned upside down. Investing your redundancy capital is about knowing what you want from it: growth, a modest income or a combination of the two. It is of paramount importance that you take impartial independent financial advice, because decisions made now can affect your finances in years to come.'
WESLEY FOX, BIRCHWOOD INVESTMENT MANAGEMENT

that you can do the kind of job in future that you have always wanted to do. You might invest your money to start your own business or buy into a business franchise, so you can feel in control of your working life once again. Or you can use the money to make appropriate financial investments to give yourself greater financial security in the future.

INVESTING YOUR REDUNDANCY MONEY – A CASE STUDY

Philip's story shows how redundancy money can be reinvested over the years to good effect. He has suffered redundancy five times during his career in purchasing. He worked as a procurement manager in the aerospace, defence, chemicals and oil industries. In most instances he found a new job quickly, which allowed him to invest most of the redundancy payments he received.

Philip was first made redundant from a job in the aerospace industry in 1971. Following the redundancy he stayed on good terms with his former employer. When the opportunity arose just a few weeks later to join a sister company (part of the same group as his former employer), he found himself having to pay that redundancy money back! The change was reclassified as an 'internal transfer' within the group. In effect, what Philip did was reinvest his redundancy money to secure a job with the sister company.

Another fifteen years into Philip's career, he found himself working in the oil industry. Eventually, the industry as a whole developed problems and shed 60,000 jobs. Because he had been judged to be a high performer, Philip was working on a special project for his employer at the time. However, it was those who were working on special projects (which were cancelled) who were made redundant while those in corporate roles kept their jobs. Life seemed very unfair. The situation turned to Philip's advantage, though. He obtained a new job in procurement in the defence industry. This meant he could invest some of the redundancy money to buy a new property. His new job meant relocating from Glasgow to Barrow-in-Furness. Several years later Philip again found himself facing redundancy. This time the cause was a company merger. His employer said 'If we're merging these three companies together, we surely don't need all these purchasing people!'

Philip was fortunate in that his employer gave him a soft landing. They provided outplacement support through Penna, a leading career transition consultancy. They helped Philip to work on his CV and provided coaching to help clarify his career options. Crucially, through them, Philip was also introduced to Wesley Fox of Birchwood Investment Management, who helped him manage the financial aspects of his redundancy.

'I remember attending a workshop Wesley ran and being impressed with him,' recalls Philip. 'Penna had organised a workshop on coping with the financial aspects of redundancy. I arranged to see a consultant who asked me a really useful question. The question he asked was "How much money could you survive on?" I gave him one figure, lower than my last salary. We discussed it and I realised the true figure was actually a lot less. So I named a new figure and we discussed it again. By the time we had finished and had discussed the shape of my finances we had a true figure, which was surprisingly small. As a result I have invested my latest redundancy payment for growth as I took a contract position.' He later took a permanent job with a consultant and then took a career break prior to retirement, keeping his options open for other occasional types of interim or consultancy roles. His investment of the money has given him greater peace of mind and greater flexibility.

Philip's advice to others in this situation is straightforward. 'If you have a problem, whether it is marital or a health problem or anything else, you need expert advice. So with a financial dilemma you need to find expert financial advice. You need to find someone you can trust.' As a procurement manager he was used to judging which consultants were trustworthy and which were not. He made a point of reading up about investment matters, so he was informed before he committed himself. He says he would advise anyone to ask themselves four questions when assessing Financial Advisers: "Are they an expert? Will they be readily available for me? Will they give me personal service? Do I trust them?" If you can answer "yes" to all of these questions, you've found someone with whom you can do business.'

25 FOLLOW YOUR PASSION

You have an opportunity now to consider your options. The best way forward could be to let yourself be led by your passion.

What is it that you love doing? What job would really excite and motivate you? Now could be the time to make it happen. The only thing holding you back could be yourself.

What distinguishes the successful entrepreneur from others? One defining characteristic is that they are enthusiastic about what they do. They love the *business* of *business*. From Richard Branson through to Duncan Bannatyne or Stelios, serial entrepreneurs believe in themselves and what they can achieve. They are passionate in pursuit of their ambitions.

Now take a long hard look at yourself. Yes, you had a job, but were you passionate about what you were doing? Was it what you talked about when you met your friends? What do you spend your spare time doing? What has given you the biggest buzz in your life? The answers may give a clue as to the most promising future direction for you in your career. If you can find a way of turning your passion into your job, you will have found yourself a new career to motivate you every single day of your life. You will have found a new career where you will be determined to succeed. You will work hard and put in long hours because it will not *feel* like work.

Sue Donnelly is a professional image coach who runs her own business, Accentuate. Sue originally ran a travel agency and has bounced back after being made redundant twice in her life. She had a dramatic 'Eureka moment' after her first meeting with a personal image trainer. She knew, at that precise moment, that this was what she wanted to do for the rest of her life. She changed career direction completely and has never looked back.

The reason for Sue's success? 'What I've done in the five years since I set up on my own, I now realise, are all the things I used to love as a child. As a child I used to spend my time endlessly playing with adult dolls, dressing them up in all kinds of different outfits. Now I do the same with adults. I used to spend lots of time as a child writing stories – now I write books on personal image issues. It's as if I've tapped into a passionate vein that was running through my entire life! It doesn't feel like work, it just feels like what I was meant to do.'

Sue's passion was fashion. What's yours?

Consider this: only a small number of British employees feel passionate about their job, yet most successful entrepreneurs are passionate about the work that they do.

Write down on a piece of paper five things you are passionate about. Then spend fifteen minutes brainstorming with your partner or a good friend to identify ways in which you could somehow turn that passion into a job.

If you are passionate about education and child-care, could you set up a nursery or out-of-school club?

If you are passionate about classic cars, could you run a club for enthusiasts, or run a business trading in classic cars, their spare parts or accessories?

If you are passionate about helping people, could you become a trainer or coach?

If you are passionate about gardening and have an eye for colour schemes, could you run your own garden design business?

If you are passionate about art, could you run an art gallery or set up a business trading in works of art?

While you do this exercise, suspend your disbelief. Allow yourself to believe it is possible. Don't veto each thought as soon as you have it by saying 'But I could never do that' or 'It's a nice idea but I'd never earn a living from it'. If you are passionate enough about it, you can find a way. Once you've had the idea, investigate it, try to talk to others who have done what you dream of doing. You'll find once you've spoken to people who have already made it happen, you begin to believe it could happen for you too.

Make passion your guide.

26 USE AN INTERIM POSITION AS A STEPPING STONE

You want a permanent full-time job, don't you? So why would you accept a temporary or part-time job? Why choose interim management, holiday or maternity cover, or a short-term contract rather than seek a longer-term role?

The answer is simple: because it can be a stepping stone that helps you on towards your goal.

'Seventy-eight per cent of those who've experienced redundancy would advise people to take a short-term or interim position rather than be out of work for long.'

REDUNDANCY TRANSFORMATIONS STUDY, ALTERNATIVE FUTURES, 2009

In the midst of a global recession, employers are understandably nervous. Companies big and small are becoming more risk-averse. They don't want to take on anyone they can't really afford, who might not turn out to be the right person for the job.

So we're seeing fewer full-time permanent jobs and more part-time, temporary jobs and short-term contracts. We're also seeing greater emphasis on outsourcing and the use of a flexible workforce of freelancers. However, companies may see employing someone on a short-term or contract basis as a good way of assessing them. If you can impress, this temporary opportunity could lead on to a permanent position. Part-time work could lead on to a full-time job.

It's easier to win a new job in an organisation from inside. If a company is downsizing and cutting down on external recruitment, it may not even advertise a new position externally. You may get to hear about it from your position on the inside. Even if the company plans to advertise the position externally, you may hear about it before they have done so. If it's a job you are qualified to do, you could save that company the cost of external advertising and a drawn-out recruitment process by quickly having a word with the right manager in that company. However, you do need to act quickly and be bold!

You can also use short-term or interim work as a way of keeping your skill set up to date, refreshing skills you haven't used for a while or gaining experience of a new industry. All of these might be important factors in helping you towards the job you really want.

27 MAKE LOOKING FOR WORK YOUR WORK

You used to have a full-time occupation, something that would occupy you from 9 to 5. You now have a new day-time schedule: the task of looking for work should occupy you full-time.

Your days need to be filled with activities that bring you closer to your next job. At this moment, you need to make looking for work your work.

> *'It is not enough to be busy – the question is, what are we busy about?'*
> HENRY DAVID THOREAU

No one should confuse activity with achievement. No one would claim that effort alone is a guarantee of success. But the opposite is certainly true: if you make no effort, you will not succeed. It is too easy to allow yourself to slip into despondency and inactivity instead of immersing yourself in the quest for a new job.

Your goal needs to be a motivating one. If your last job didn't excite, challenge and develop you, you are hardly likely to be motivated to find another job that is just the same. Begin by having a goal worth pursuing. Visualise yourself in the right job – one that meets all your emotional as well as financial needs. That job is your goal. It may be a very different job from the last one you had. Now you can strain every sinew and the effort will be worth it, because the prize you have visualised is worth pursuing.

'You're wasting your time– no one spends seven or eight hours a day looking for work', you might hear people say. 'It only takes a few hours at most to send off job applications. Besides, there are no jobs to be found in your industry or your kind of role right now. It's all futile.' However, these are the voices of the difficulty-staters of this world, people who won't make the effort to make things happen but will readily pour cold water on the hopes of others. Don't listen to these voices. Don't become one of them.

If there really are no jobs in your field or industry right now and no real prospects for the future, you will need to retrain for a new career or start your own business. It's going to be as simple as that! You might modify your financial situation by downshifting and look to earn income in different ways. You will certainly need to find a way to change your life significantly and you will need to act quickly.

Make sure you approach looking for work with the same commitment and focus that you employed in your job.

The lack of jobs is not an excuse for doing nothing – it is a call to action! If this is honestly the situation you face, waste no time in changing direction. Try to identify which sectors have jobs available and spot which types of job you might do (with and without retraining). Jobs you have the aptitude to do. Jobs you have the enthusiasm to do. Are you really saying you can't imagine spending seven hours a day researching other careers, speaking to people in those other industries, taking training courses to equip you with the skills you need and networking with others who might help you find jobs? Of course you can! In fact, you start to realise that seven hours a day might not be enough.

What if there are some jobs in your chosen career but they are few and far between? This means you should redouble your efforts to hear about all the jobs that are going, as soon as you possibly can.

The importance of networking actively can't be overstated. Many jobs simply aren't advertised. Your goal must be to hear about these possible opportunities, if possible before the decisions are taken by the employer to advertise them. If you can approach an employer directly to offer yourself as the answer to their problem before the job has even been advertised, you may be in luck. You might save them the time and the cost of advertising, and make that job your own – at least on a temporary or trial basis. Your support group (the collection of friends, relatives and former colleagues that you have put together) will act as 'eyes and ears' for you in your job search. You in return should do everything in your power to help them in their lives.

Make sure you are registered with the right recruitment consultancies and ensure they have the most up-to-date copy of your CV. Build a relationship with your recruitment consultancy. Keep in regular contact with them and keep your name at the front of their minds. Monitor the jobs websites and make sure you are registered with all of the right ones.

If jobs are scarce, it is more important than ever for your application to stand out from the crowd. Efforts made to polish your CV may pay off. Efforts to improve your interview skills, so you can shine at interview, may also reap dividends. Practise your interview skills with a friend, taking turns to play the roles of employer and candidate.

To make looking for work your work requires a shift in mindset. Each day must have one clear goal: to bring you closer to your next job. A clear focus coupled with tenacity will win you that job. Don't be disheartened and don't ever give up!

28 GO FREELANCE

Become a 'flea on the back of an elephant'! Large companies may want to employ you, but only on a flexible basis. They may be willing to pay you, but not have you on their payroll.

You can learn to live off them without belonging to them. If you have a professional skill you could become a successful freelancer earning your income working with a variety of firms.

Just because companies are downsizing doesn't mean their needs have disappeared. Often the act of downsizing will have left them worse off. As a company they still have significant needs but now lack enough internal staff with the skills to address them. The answer for many companies is to give work to an army of freelancers who they can call on as necessary to perform particular tasks.

Charles Handy's famous book *The Elephant and the Flea: Reflections of a Reluctant Capitalist* describes how the business world has been changing over the years. We're moving towards a world where workers are more independent and flea-like, flitting from job to job, latching on to elephants (large corporations) whenever they need to.

'Only one manager in ten considers freelancing after being made redundant. Yet it can be a productive route in to a new job and not just a stop-gap measure.'
REDUNDANCY TRANSFORMATIONS STUDY, ALTERNATIVE FUTURES, 2009

'Freelancing can be a good way in, especially for the older person who may perhaps not seem as attractive to an employer at first. If you go freelance, an employer can get an impression of you – and you of them – without a long-term commitment'
KATE FARRINGTON, PRINCIPAL CAREER CONSULTANT, PENNA

If you have a professional skill you could soon find yourself in demand as a freelancer. It could be a more stimulating and varied time than you've enjoyed in your working life so far!

FREELANCING – A CASE STUDY

Here's one story of how easily the transition can occur. Graham Sharp went from being Deputy Managing Director of an advertising agency to become a successful market research freelancer. He didn't initially intend to become self-employed, it just turned out that way. And it turned out to be a lifestyle he was ideally suited for.

'My advertising agency was taken over by an international marketing communications group. In the aftermath of this, the message came through from our new owners that we had to reduce our costs. Firstly I had to make people redundant, which was a really unpleasant thing to have to do. Then, as the market became much tougher, it was my turn to be made redundant too.

'At first I made the big mistake of looking for another job which was just the same, trying to replace the job I'd lost. I spent over six months looking for other advertising agency jobs. I found some of the worst recruitment agencies *pigeonhole* you – they only consider you for jobs which are identical to the one you lost. So I applied for jobs directly. I went for a job with one advertising agency and they invited me back for a second and then a third interview. By the time we got to the third interview I was pretty confident I'd got the job, I thought the third interview would just be discussing what colour of car I wanted. But they came back after it and said, "Terribly sorry, but it's a no".

'But I kept talking to people at the ad·agency even after they'd rejected me. They said they had a couple of research projects they'd like me to manage. So I worked from home on these two projects, which led on to several more. After another year of working with me on a freelance basis, they said "We realise we made a mistake turning you down, would you like to come and work for us full-time?" But by that time I had gone down a different road and had a number of different clients all giving me freelance projects.

'I still remember my "Road to Damascus" moment. It came when I'd been working as a freelancer for about six months. I suddenly realised that getting a new job wasn't the only way to make a good living. I had a substantial amount of freelance work by then and I was earning more than I would have done if I had been employed. And enjoying it more!

'When I started to work freelance, I wasn't thinking of starting a business. What I was doing, in my own mind, was demonstrating my capabilities to lots of potential employers in the hope one of them would be so impressed with my freelance work that they'd offer me a full-time job. As I've said, a job offer was forthcoming, so my plan worked really well – but by then I'd decided I preferred being a freelancer!

'I've now been working as a freelancer for over fifteen years. I love it. I have flexibility in my life, I can accept the work I want and occasionally turn down work I don't want. I choose my own hours, to a large extent. I work from home or my office, or from client premises – whichever is appropriate. People say to me "Don't you miss the job security of working for a large company?", but the truth is I feel that I have more job security now than I had then. My job isn't dependent on the performance of a single company. I have a dozen clients, businesses which support me and operate in different market sectors. Even if some of these businesses run into financial difficulties, my business can still do well.'

Could you be a successful freelancer too?

29 SET UP YOUR OWN BUSINESS AS A SOLE TRADER

Here's a thought. You don't need an employer to give you a job. You can become self-employed.

Setting up in business as a sole trader is the simplest way to go into business for yourself. There are more than two million sole traders in business today – individuals working for themselves. They make up two-thirds of the small businesses in this country. So why not you?

Many people dream of being their own boss but never do it. Forty-three per cent of Britons have dreamed about starting up their own business according to a recent survey by One Life. It seems easier to get a job with someone else, yet it may not be, particularly during a recession when employers are shedding staff not taking them on. If the jobs on offer are in short supply, why not employ yourself?

If you have a talent or skill or knowledge that someone else needs and is willing to pay for, you could run a successful sole trader business. You could take the first steps to set up your business today and be working for yourself next week. It can be as easy and quick as that! What have you got to lose?

Sole traders are the main kind of business in Britain. Here are some of the main kinds of activities that lend themselves to freelance or individual sole trader operations:

- Trades: carpenter, decorator, plumber, window cleaner, cleaner, gardener.
- Management: accountant, researcher, consultant.
- IT: computing support, website design.
- Health and beauty: holistic therapist, hairdresser.
- Administration: outsourced secretarial and administrative services.
- Personal tuition: teachers of music, maths, languages, cookery.
- Coaching: life coaching, small business coaching, personal image coaching.

Many of these sole trader businesses are services that can be offered working from home. So business overheads (fixed costs) are minimal. Here are a couple of myths I've found about running your own small business:

'As many as one person in four considers setting up their own business after being made redundant – but only one person in every ten goes on to do it.'
REDUNDANCY TRANSFORMATIONS SURVEY, ALTERNATIVE FUTURES, 2009

- *It'll be lonely working alone.* Not true. You need to be continually making connections, meeting people and talking to people to help you win the business, service the customers and fulfil the tasks you are set. You also need to organise administrative, technical and accountancy support for your business. You will probably see more people than ever. It is anything but lonely!
- *I'll be distracted by other things working from home.* Not true, although you need to be disciplined to make it so. Running your own business will be hard work if you are to be successful. It's a good idea to set aside separate space within your home (an office, study, loft or converted garage) to be your work space and minimise distractions.

One step to take before you set up your own business as a sole trader is to go to a workshop on starting your own business. Business Link, the government-funded support service to help new businesses thrive, provides free workshops on how to get started. Your bank will also be happy to give you free advice about setting up a business.

Once you've been on a Business Link introductory workshop, you'll know what you need to do to set up in business as a sole trader. It is quite easy – the practicalities and legal requirements are relatively few. For instance, you need to register yourself as a sole trader and decide what to call yourself (your own name is enough if you don't want to be creative). You need to decide whether you're likely to earn enough to require VAT registration. You will want to set up a separate business bank account and may want to put a little cash of your own into it as a personal loan to get it started. This can be drawn back later. You may need to arrange special business insurance policies such as Public Liability Insurance (covering you for any accidental damage you might make to a client's property or possessions) and Professional Indemnity Insurance (covering you against any lapses of professional competence). These can be combined in a single policy. But be wary about adding costs to your business before you've earned any money!

After perhaps a week or two of preparation, you can be in business as a sole trader. If you have set it up carefully it may be difficult for this business to lose money – for instance, you might resolve not to draw any earnings from the business until after you've been paid.

So why not try setting yourself up your own business as a sole trader and check out whether this works for you? You may surprise yourself. You'll learn new things along the way, make new connections and earn some extra money. If after trying it you discover it's not for you, you will still have gained a new and valuable experience in your life!

30 SET UP YOUR OWN BUSINESS AS A PARTNERSHIP OR LIMITED COMPANY

Choosing the correct legal status for your business can be tricky, but there are plenty of good sources of advice.

You'll also need some help with forecasting cash flow and formulating your business plans. Talking to your business coach, Business Link and to your bank at an early stage is a wise move.

If you're starting up your own business, its legal status is something you need to sort out at the very beginning. Should you be a sole trader or form a limited company, a partnership or a limited liability partnership? If in doubt, you might always start as a sole trader and evolve your business later into another form. Talk to your small business coach about this decision, if you have one. Business Link provides free seminars for those thinking of starting up their own business. If you're not sure what is best to do, why not talk to them first?

Your bank will also be able to advise you. Banks often provide factsheets and face-to-face advice for customers who are thinking of starting their own business. Since your bank will be a crucial business partner moving forward, it is a good idea to speak to them and seek their advice at an early stage. NatWest is a leading UK bank that is giving extra support nowadays to new business start-ups. According to NatWest, 'we've found that financial worries are the main reason customers give for not turning their idea into a business. So what we're doing is providing each new small business customer with two years' free banking and a dedicated Business Manager based at their local branch. More than 1,000 NatWest relationship managers are on hand to help startup customers in all the important areas, including managing cash flow, planning, risk management and marketing.'

Before you get moving with all this, you need to decide what your business will offer, what to call it and determine its legal status. A quick summary of the main choices available are:

- *Sole trader* – the simplest way of running a business. It consists of an individual working alone, such as a freelancer. The person *is* the business. You get to keep all the profits personally but the downside is that you are also personally liable for all debts.
- *Partnership* – two or more individuals collaborating and sharing the costs and risks of running a business. All partners register as self-employed and take a share in the profits. Creditors can make a claim against any of the partners. So you really are in it together!
- *Limited company* – a company such as XYZ Ltd that exists as a separate legal entity in its own right and where the company's finances are separate from the personal finances of the company's owners. Shareholders are not normally responsible for the company's debts. The company can be bought and sold. Limited companies need to be registered at Companies House.
- *Limited liability partnership* – a company such as XYZ LLP, similar to an ordinary partnership in that a number of individuals together share in the risks and rewards. However, the liability is limited, so that members have some protection if the business runs into trouble.

It's not inevitable that if you are operating alone you should set up as a sole trader. Sometimes you might operate alone on a day-to-day basis, but still choose to set up a limited company. You need someone else, though, to act as your Company Secretary. That's a legal requirement.

CHOOSING WHICH TYPE OF BUSINESS TO SET UP – CASE STUDIES

When Phil was made redundant from his job in a leading investment bank, he received outplacement support from Penna, including a number of one-to-one coaching sessions and workshops. He decided to set up a consultancy working in financial services and other sectors, including the not-for-profit sector. He decided to do this as a limited company rather than as a sole trader. Phil explains: 'a limited company conveys a certain cachet and gravitas, so I was leaning towards this anyway. I found that for certain interim management positions and longer-term consultancy deals – certainly those over six months – they tend only to consider you if you have set yourself up as a limited company. I believe this is for tax reasons.'

When Jane Francis was made redundant from her job as a senior product manager in the Marketing Department of a major insurance company, she fell into freelance work almost immediately. Her husband worked for a marketing consultancy and they needed freelance support. Jane had just had a baby and wasn't looking for full-time work, so this arrangement suited her well. Soon it became regular freelance support, three days a week. Her legal status at the time was as a sole trader. However when her husband Mike, left the company, Jane and Mike decided to set up their own marketing consultancy, this time as a partnership.

'We wanted it to be a partnership in every sense of the word,' says Jane. 'Our skills dovetail very well. Mike is very clear-minded and steady of purpose, very self-motivated, and we'd worked together before. I knew we would be a successful team.' Choosing to run a business with your life partner is not without its challenges. But as Jane says, 'it was far easier for me to contemplate running a business together with Mike than with anyone else. If you're going into business with a partner, you need to know them very well. You need to trust them completely with the financial side of things. You need to be complementary characters, rather than duplicating the same set of skills. And you need to have the same long-term goals. On that basis, I really couldn't imagine going into business with anyone other than my husband.'

According to a recent survey by One Life Live, 43 per cent of Britons dream of starting their own business. Nowadays that dream is as likely to be starting an IT consultancy business or a creative design agency as running a shop. Britain is no longer just a nation of shop-keepers! What kind of business might you start?

31 INVEST IN A FRANCHISE

If you want to be your own boss and have money to invest, the easiest way to get started may be to buy a franchise. You operate under an established brand or company name, using a proven business model. And you get to run it yourself – although you'll find you have to work to set procedures and standards set out in the franchise agreement.

Got the get-up-and-go to be your own boss? Have you received a large redundancy cheque from your former employer that would otherwise get frittered away over the next year or two? Are you keen to take up a new challenge, to do something different right now? Do you like the idea of running your own business but you're still not sure what and would feel uncertain about doing it alone?

A business franchise could be the answer. There are thousands of franchise opportunities available. Franchise owners are always looking to expand their businesses by bringing in new managers to run franchise operations. Some of the biggest brand names are actually franchise operations. The most famous franchise of all is probably McDonald's restaurants, although managing a McDonald's restaurant wouldn't be for everyone. Other famous franchises include ActionCoach (business coaching), Bairstow Eves (estate agents), Cartridge World (printing refills), ChipsAway (car repairs), Coffee Republic (coffee shops), Clarks (retailer of shoes), Domino's Pizza (restaurant), Kall Kwik (printing), Molly Maid (cleaning), Pitman Training (training colleges for office skills), Rosemary Conley (diet and fitness clubs), Scottish & Newcastle (pubs), Stagecoach (theatre schools), TaxAssist (accountants) and Western Provident Association (medical insurance). There are franchise operations covering just about every business sector that you might want to get into!

Banks are more likely to lend to you as a franchisee than for a small business idea you have developed yourself. This is because as a franchisee you are working to a well-defined, proven business model. They know you can be successful because that business model has a proven track record of success. The franchisor will give you examples of what you can hope to earn and introduce you to people who are running their existing franchises successfully.

As a general rule you'll need *at least* £20,000 (sometimes significantly more for retail-based franchises) to invest in a franchise. This payment will cover your initial franchise fee. This money pays for you to buy the licence to operate under that brand for a particular length of time, for instance five years. There will probably be geographical restrictions on your franchise: you might be buying the right to operate under that brand in a particular town or region of the country, for instance. The cost of franchises varies significantly and there are a few franchises (often for home-based roles) that cost a great deal less than this. You'll also have ongoing management services charges to pay: typically you pay the franchisor a specified percentage of your turnover. You may be bound by your contract to purchase all supplies in future from the franchisor, for example if you are running a restaurant or a coffee shop.

In return, you will get to operate under an established brand that is being supported by central advertising and promotional activity. You'll receive comprehensive training plus ongoing management support. You may get support for central services such as finance or HR, so you're not hassled by invoicing or employee contracts.

Of course, in the first instance you need to be accepted by the franchisor as a suitable person to run a franchise for their brand. They will have quality control measures in place to ensure you fulfil your side of the bargain and don't damage their brand. Just because you have the money to do it, you can't assume you will be accepted to run a franchise. But there are hundreds of franchises out there to be run. Franchisors want to find people who have management expertise, motivation and money to invest. They want to expand their businesses by bringing in new people like you! Since you are paying for the franchise, the balance of power is certainly different from an employer-employee relationship. You're not asking them to give you a job, you're investing in a business opportunity with them as your business partner.

Banks will be more likely to lend to you as a franchisee than for a small business idea you've developed yourself, because a franchisee is operating a proven business model.

What's the downside? Well, obviously the cost can be a big barrier. Be sure you understand the ongoing cash requirements of the business and don't make the common mistake of underestimating these. Buying a franchise is not a move to be taken lightly. You need to do careful research first. For those of a creative bent, the restrictions and quality control measures in the franchise agreement can be a challenge. You won't have the freedom to innovate that would come from having created your own business. You need to follow fixed processes and procedures. It's also a significant tie: you are committing to doing this for a specified period. Be sure you understand the exit routes before you walk in the entry door.

If you think franchising appeals to you, the best first steps are to:

- read a magazines such as *FranchiseWorld* or *The Franchise Magazine*
- check out various franchising websites such as the British Franchise Association (the BFA also runs low-cost seminars about franchising)
- visit a franchising exhibition such as the British and International Franchise Exhibition, and speak to experts on franchising.

Make sure that you've spoken to several people who are already part of the franchise network for that business before you commit to taking one up. Understand the practical challenges you are likely to face. It will be hard work. You will need to be determined and committed to make it work. However, for some, this chance to run a business using an established brand, a proven business model and with central training and support, will be exactly what they want.

Franchising may be a simple and bold way for you to overcome redundancy!

32 CLOSE THE BOOK

This chapter of your life has ended. It's time to close the book and place it firmly back on the bookshelf. It's time to look forwards, not backwards.

Repeatedly thinking about what's happened, endlessly dwelling on it, will not help you move forward. It will prevent you from making progress.

You can't move forwards if you are looking backwards. Sometimes an event occurs in your life that is deeply upsetting. It is so dramatic and traumatic that it fills your thoughts, quite understandably, for some time. At all kinds of odd moments, the memories and thoughts come unbidden into your mind.

> *'Things turn out best for the people who make the best of the way things turn out.'*
> ART LINKLETTER

Perhaps your experience of the day you heard about your redundancy was like that? At the time you might have felt anger, resentment, bitterness, shock, cynicism and a host of other negative feelings. Perhaps those feelings are still intense right now? You might have a short film playing repeatedly in your mind of the moment you were told the news. You may still be inwardly replaying the words your employer used to tell you about the redundancy. Perhaps they didn't phrase things as delicately or carefully as they should and now you feel angry, discarded and undervalued?

But if you keep listening to that soundtrack, you will do yourself no favours. If you keep reading these few pages from the Book of Your Life, you will be dragged down. You will find yourself falling victim to self-pity and depression, rather than facing the future with optimism and a new sense of mission.

So it is time to learn how to close the book. Call up a powerful mental image, the image of closing a book and replacing it firmly on the shelf. You can use this mental image to help yourself through these testing times.

Imagine that the book contains the story of your redundancy. You can choose when to pick it up and read from it and when to put it down.

In the early days, immediately after you have been made redundant, it is simply unreasonable to ask yourself to stop thinking about it. The best way through initially is to find a way to release your emotions. Release that pressure valve: let it all out, quickly. You may need to find a particularly good friend who is willing to listen to you sounding off for a while, before gently bringing you back to where you are and the practical steps you can take to move forward. Tell your friend you need to say what's on your mind and ask them if they'd be good enough to listen. Let it all out and then leave it behind.

If you keep reading those few pages from the Book of Your Life you will be dragged down. So close the book!

Thereafter, if you find negative thoughts and memories coming into your mind unbidden, summon up the image of the book. Picture yourself reading from it in your mind. See yourself in your mind decisively closing that book and placing it back on the shelf.

If you find you can't keep these thoughts out completely, decide to allow yourself to read that book for only a certain time each day – only between 9 a.m. and 10 a.m., for instance. Make that the only time you will permit yourself the indulgence of looking backwards and reliving the trauma of redundancy. At all other hours of the day, negativity should be banned. The book should remain firmly on the bookshelf.

There's another book waiting to be looked at: the Book of Your Future Life. At the moment its pages are blank. What gets written on those pages is up to you. You can't help where you are now in the story, but you can decide what happens next.

33   REASSESS YOUR PRIORITIES IN LIFE

Was your last job bringing you health, wealth and happiness? If the stress or the long working hours were killing you, if the financial rewards weren't what you wanted, if you weren't getting the recognition you deserved, if you weren't enjoying getting up to go to work in the mornings, now is the time to reassess your priorities.

You don't have to wait until you are on your deathbed to conduct a life review. Now is as good a time as any for that!

Spend an hour or two looking back on your life and career so far. Be honest with yourself. Is what you've been doing what you always hoped you'd do? Have you been fulfilled by what you were doing with your life? Are you content with what you have achieved?

If the answer to any of these questions is 'no', then maybe you should reassess your priorities in life. Our priorities in life aren't really demonstrated by what we say but by what we do. What are the tasks we devote our time to and what do we exclude?

There is the story that has been handed down that goes something like this. A hard-working executive was working in his study at home at the weekend. It was a Sunday and he was desperately catching up on his work. He had a busy week ahead so he was also preparing for some international business meetings he had coming up. His young daughter came into the room. 'What's that, Daddy?' she asked, pointing at his diary with its list of business meetings.

'Oh, that's just a list of all the important people Daddy has to meet in the next week,' he answered.

'Am I on that list, Daddy?' she asked. Result: one humbled father.

What are your life's priorities? Ask yourself these questions: 'If I were looking back on my life right now, if that was it for me, what would I regret not doing?' or 'When my life is over, what would I like to be remembered for?' The answers may tell you a lot about yourself and your true priorities.

It may be time to select a new trajectory for your life and create a new endpoint.

> *'When we are behaving mindlessly, that is to say, relying on categories drawn in the past, endpoints to development seem fixed. We are then like projectiles moving along a predetermined course. When we are mindful, we see all sorts of choices and generate new endpoints.'*
> ELLEN J. LANGER

According to the Redundancy Transformations Study by Alternative Futures, two-thirds of people who experience redundancy say it is the spur for them to make major changes in their lives. Maybe it is time to be more mindful of the important things, the things that really matter to you? If you haven't done so already in your life, perhaps now is the moment to start to listen to your true motivations?

For some these deliberations will spur them on to even greater success in exactly the same field as they were previously. Because sometimes the reaction to rejection is to think, 'I'll show them!' Would it not be supremely satisfying to work for a company that outperformed your old company? That overtook them in terms of market share?

For others, the impact of these reassessments will lead them into a decisive shift towards independence. Moving out of the corporate world and saying hello to self-employment. Waving goodbye to office politics.

Becoming their own boss and choosing their own direction. Taking responsibility for their own future employment and earnings. Making sure no one ever makes them redundant ever again. The purpose of that work, the subject for their business, can be whatever they want it to be, so long as they can make it work.

And for you? Does a reassessment of your life's priorities lead you towards a new career, or to further advancement within your current career? Does it lead you to more of the same or to a very different work-life balance? Do you feel drawn towards a single-track route forward (a single career) or a portfolio career, where several tracks run in parallel? Or does it lead you to move away from materialism and embrace a simpler lifestyle?

'Whether you chose your change or not, there are unlived potentialities within you, interests and talents that you have not yet explored. Transitions clear the ground for new growth. They drop the curtain so that the stage can be set for a new scene. What is it, at this point in your life, that is waiting quietly backstage for an entrance cue?'
WILLIAM BRIDGES

Only you can answer these questions. Only you can judge whether the change that takes place in your life at the moment is going to be played in a major or minor key. As William Bridges pertinently asked, 'What is it, at this point in your life, that is waiting quietly backstage for an entrance cue?'

It may have been waiting patiently backstage for a long time. Are you going to make that call?

34 GIVE YOURSELF A FRESH IMAGE

The image you convey is incredibly important. Whether you are hoping to shine at a job interview or you are starting up your own business and trying to win clients, you need to project the right image.

'Communication is 55% appearance, 38% tone, 7% words.'
ALBERT MEHRABIAN, THE SILENT REPORT

Take a good look at yourself in the mirror. It may be time for a new look, a new image – a new you!

Here's a thought. At a job interview your prospective employers will typically have made up their mind about you within five minutes of your arrival. They'll do so on the basis of both verbal and non-verbal communication. As everyone has probably heard by now, more than 90% of all communication is non-verbal. Your appearance, your body language and your clothes are all sending messages to others about you. Even when employers weigh up your answers to interview questions, how you said it could be as important as what you said. So you do need to think about your tone of voice, the confidence with which you speak, the clarity and pace of what you say.

Image is a double influence. The way you look will affect how people react to you and also affect how confident you feel when you speak.

Leading image coach Sue Donnelly is President of the Federation of Image Consultants. She also runs her own image consultancy, Accentuate. Her view on personal image is that 'it should be the first thing people think about if they want to relaunch themselves – nothing is more important when it comes to increasing your self-confidence'.

Sue herself bounced back from redundancy (she has been made redundant twice in her career) when she finally discovered her niche and set up her own image consultancy business. She is now a published author, with books such as *Feel Fab at Fifty*, is a regular conference speaker and is author of numerous magazine articles on personal image and impact.

Here's Sue's advice. 'If you're going for a job interview, be aware that first impressions matter enormously. The way you dress needs to communicate your personality. Take care of the small as well as the large details. Make sure your hair is styled to suit you, that your shoes aren't scuffed and that your fingernails are neat. You need to dress for your audience expectations, but you also need to be authentic. If the two don't match up, then you really do need to think whether you're right for the job!

'A new outfit for an interview will obviously lift your spirits – but make sure you choose it yourself and you feel good in it. You should have already worn the outfit a couple of times so that you feel comfortable and relaxed in it. You can then concentrate on the job in hand rather than your clothes.

'Think also about whether your clothes communicate that you are powerful or approachable. In general, approachability is going to be communicated by more colourful outfits, greater use of patterns and softer fabrics. Power is communicated by more sober outfits that use fewer colours and patterns. What message do you want your audience to receive?'

> *'In our view, top employers want to see someone who is smartly dressed and smart – someone who is confident in their own skin and dresses in the style which is expected for the role. You can't win a job solely by the way you look, but you can certainly lose it.'*
> KATE FARRINGTON, PRINCIPAL CAREER CONSULTANT, PENNA

If you can look the part on arrival at interview, you've crossed the first hurdle.

Think about what you'd like a prospective employer to be saying about you after your job interview. Then ask a trusted friend what your clothes and appearance say about you. Encourage them to be totally honest and forthright. If the employer wants someone who is self-confident, personable, opinionated and a go-getter, but your clothes and appearance are shouting 'Quiet, conservative, shy', then you simply aren't going to get that job.

For men this can be a particularly difficult point to take on board. Many men, particularly those who've been with a single employer for a long time, may have stopped thinking too hard about the suit they put on every morning, or their overall look. They may have stopped thinking about the image they convey through the way they dress. Any step that they take to lift their image will pay dividends in raising their confidence.

35 FIND YOUR INNER CALM

This is a stressful time, but don't panic. Things will sort themselves out, but for the time being you need to find a way to take stress out of the situation and keep yourself calm through this challenge.

The time immediately after being made redundant can be one of the most stressful times in your life, if you allow it to be. It is quite normal to feel anxious, confused, upset and stressed. You need to take steps to minimise that stress.

Getting your finances in order is an important step. Working out exactly what you have coming in and going out each month. Working out what you need to pay and when. Working out how long your redundancy payment (if you were lucky enough to have one) plus your savings will last. If you know the facts about your situation, you may be able to tell yourself something like 'I have twelve months' breathing space to find a new job'.

You'll find it a lot less stressful if you can begin to form contingency plans and talk to others about them. Put a few marker points down on the timeline. Establish the facts and then try to say things like:

- 'I'll give it six months and if I haven't found a job by then, I'll put the house on the market and downsize.'
- 'If after nine months I haven't found a permanent job, I'll look for a temporary job.'

- 'I'll sign up for this training for the next three months and then throw my hat back in the ring by registering with recruitment consultants.'

What this kind of thinking is doing is putting you in the driving seat. It's putting you back in control. We all feel particularly stressed by situations that are beyond our control. The moment you accept the facts and articulate a plan is the moment you start to feel on top of the situation. That's when the stress and tension will begin to slip away.

Make a conscious effort to unwind. Make time in your life, each day, for little things that you know help you to relax. Set aside half-an-hour or an hour to yourself each day, when you can go for a walk, have a relaxing bath, read a book or sit and meditate – whatever works for you. Look for an activity that you know relaxes you the most and build it into your daily programme. If you have a pet (particularly a dog or a cat), you'll find them a great aid to relaxation. If you haven't, perhaps you have a friend or neighbour who owns a dog – you might help out by taking their dog on walks.

Look for the activity that you know relaxes you the most and build it into your daily programme.

Music can be greatly soothing. Set aside time to listen to the type of music that will relax you. Art too can allow you to express your emotions and is a way of getting rid of angst.

If you have friends who can help you, engage them on some reciprocal basis. Say you're a keen gardener but you have a friend who is a reflexologist. Do a trade: you do some gardening for them; they provide a foot massage to help you unwind.

Make a point of being open and honest about your situation and your feelings with your family and friends. They will support you, but you need to let them know how you feel. Don't hide behind a façade. The worst thing you can do is bottle up your feelings and pretend to be unaffected when inside you are hurting. That's the way to send your stress levels through the roof!

Find your inner peace. This situation was not of your making. It's not your fault. The job was made redundant, not you. Your previous employer didn't want to make you redundant, it was simply responding to difficult economic circumstances. It wasn't personal, so there's no need to bear your previous employer any ill will. Don't be angry and bitter – this will only make you feel tense. Pick yourself up, dust yourself down and move on.

Finally, remember that two-thirds of all people whose lives are changed by redundancy find that their lives are ultimately changed for the better. It's just the transitional stage – where you are right now – that is difficult. If you keep calm you will find things improve as you emerge at a better place in your life. Personally you will have learned a lot about yourself too.

Resolve to pass through this transitional phase without regrets and with a minimum of stress.

36 PRACTISE YOUR INTERVIEW TECHNIQUE

'Practice makes perfect,' they say. Yet many people walk into job interviews without having practised at all!

Job interviews aren't easy to come by, so you owe it to yourself to prepare properly. Yes, there will be some questions you can't predict, but there are others you can reasonably assume will be asked.

You can significantly increase your chances of getting a job by polishing your interview technique and rehearsing before the performance. If you were in your last job for a long time, it may be many years since you have been in a job interview. So you need to think how to put yourself across in the best way. It is important to prepare for every interview in the same thorough way, whether it is with a recruitment consultant, executive search agency or an employer.

There are two ways of practising. The first approach is visualisation: a mental rehearsal. Picture the possible interview scene in your mind. Use any information you have been given in advance about the interview, plus the power of your own imagination. Imagine how the interview room might look. How many people are there? Is your future line manager or the HR manager interviewing you, or both? Are they sitting across a desk from you?

Try to visualise this as clearly as possible. Now imagine yourself being shown into that interview room and being asked to take a seat. Picture yourself as strong and confident, making eye contact with your interviewers, establishing immediate rapport. It is vital in this visualisation that you see things *going well*. If something goes wrong in your mental picture, play the scene again but this time with a positive outcome. Imagine the small talk at the very beginning about your journey to the interview or the weather. See yourself smiling confidently.

Now imagine the warm-up questions. Most interviews will begin with some gentle questioning to get the interviewee talking and to relax them. They

'Most employers make up their mind about a candidate within five minutes of the start of a job interview.'

KATE FARRINGTON, PRINCIPAL CAREER CONSULTANT, PENNA

might be asking you how you chose this career in the first place – what first interested you to about this particular industry? The interview will be mainly open questions that require far more than a 'yes' or 'no' answer. In this visualisation exercise, see yourself mirroring the pace and style of the interviewer. If they have a slow and calm delivery, you are answering slowly and calmly. If they have a quick-fire delivery, you are answering rapidly. See yourself mirroring their body language a little. If they gesture with their hands, you are communicating with your hands too. Mirroring is a powerful technique from NLP (neuro-linguistic programming) that helps to establish rapport. These early moments in an interview are particularly important: many employers make up their minds about a candidate within five minutes of the start of a job interview.

Now rehearse in your mind some of the tougher questions you'll be asked. How did you feel about being made redundant? What is the biggest challenge you've faced in your career and how did you deal with it? These are the kinds of questions that directly or indirectly bring your recent experience of redundancy into the conversation. You want to show through your answers that you have faced up to the shock and disappointment and have moved on. You have treated the redundancy as a challenge to be overcome.

Expect to be questioned too on whether you are applying for different types of job. This is difficult to answer as you don't want to imply that you are anything less than committed to this particular job. Questions like 'What other roles are you considering right now?' or 'How will you know when you've found the right job?' can be difficult questions. Make sure your references to other possible directions are in the past tense. You need to come across as knowing your own mind: you know this job, with this company, is the one for you!

Once you've carried out the mental visualisation exercise several times, it is time to practise with a trusted friend. Roleplay the interview. Your friend can play the part of the interviewer, asking a number of questions that you've written down for them. Let your friend also ask any supplementary questions they want to at the time. Discuss in advance the kind of personal qualities and experience the employer is likely to be looking for. Afterwards, review the roleplay with your friend. Get their feedback on which answers came across well and which ones didn't. Repeat the roleplay until you feel comfortable with your answers to the kinds of questions you are anticipating.

Here are some well-known difficult interview questions:

- 'Why do you want to work for this company?' (You need to have done your research on that company in advance.)
- 'What are your biggest strengths?' (Easy, but of course it leads on to the 'noose question' …) '… And what are your biggest weaknesses?'
- 'What's your greatest personal achievement in your life so far?'
- 'Tell us about a time when you've had to deal with a very tight deadline (or a stressful situation) and how you handled it?'
- 'What sort of tasks do you find difficult?'
- 'What is the one thing your working colleagues would like to change about you?'
- 'How have you been spending your time whilst you've been unemployed?'
- 'Where do you see yourself in five years' time?'

You'll find it helpful to prepare some answers in advance to these types of questions!

37   BE FOCUSED

The greater clarity you can have about your goal, the more successful you will be. If you can achieve clarity then you can visualise success. You can focus.

Top athletes will use one word repeatedly in interviews. That word is 'focus'. With focus comes drive and determination. They have clarity of purpose. Diversionary activities that clutter their lives and don't contribute to their main goal can be avoided.

No one gets to be a top athlete without dedication. Hours of practice, day after day. Whether they feel in the mood or not. Whether they feel on top form or not. Every day, top athletes will follow their daily training regime. What helps them maintain their motivation through all of this is their focus. They have a strong vision of

'Nothing can add more power to your life than concentrating all of your energies on a limited set of targets.'
NIDO QUBEIN, MOTIVATIONAL SPEAKER

the end goal. Perhaps their aim is to win a gold medal at the Olympics, or to represent their country at a particular event, or simply to achieve a personal best at a particular athletics event. The goal is clear. It is tangible and time-limited. It can be easily visualised. All of this helps to increase focus. Ask yourself: would an athlete without focus be successful?

So how can you be focused right now?

At the moment you may have a myriad of future possibilities swirling around in your mind. Should you retrain? Should you look for an interim position? Should you start your own business? There are many future directions you might take and at this moment you might not know which one will be the best route to take.

Here's a suggestion. Begin by drawing up a simple four-point schedule. The timings must be based on what you know about your practical situation, for instance your financial situation. You've worked out how long your redundancy money will last and you know you need to make things happen within that timeframe.

1 Point 1 on your schedule might be labelled 'Thinking time'. You might choose to give yourself a few months for this, depending on your situation. During this period you will take time to think through your situation, take stock of your options, talk to trusted friends and colleagues, meet with professional advisers, and research other careers and possibilities.

2 Point 2 on your schedule could be labelled 'Determine direction'. This is your moment of choice. The time you decide on your goal. The direction you are now going to select, from amongst all of your options. Choose well. Don't leap to a choice too early, but don't delay making that choice simply because you are afraid to.

3 Point 3 on your schedule could read 'Making it happen'. List the actions you will take to move towards that goal. Other than generic actions, such as networking, this section will be largely blank at first until your goal has been determined. You can begin to fill in the detail against this point in the schedule as your future direction becomes clearer.

4 Point 4, the final entry on your schedule, could be labelled 'Arrival'. When do you need to have arrived at your destination? Working back from this, what timings do you need to have against points 1, 2 and 3?

See if you can create in your mind, as early as possible, an image of yourself at this arrival point in the future. There you are, actually doing this job. If your goal is to retrain as a teacher, you might see an image of yourself standing in the classroom, addressing the students. Hold that picture in your mind as firmly as possible. Try to imagine what it would feel like, what sort of thing you might say, so that your image is as complete as possible.

Great buildings are created twice; once in the imagination and once in practice. An architect will prepare detailed technical drawings of the building before it is built. No great building could be created without this kind of vision in advance, a clear picture of what it will ultimately look like. Could the Pyramids, the Eiffel Tower, the Taj Mahal or St Paul's Cathedral have been built without a plan, without a vision?

You may need to be patient in achieving that vision. The Redundancy Transformations Study by Alternative Futures shows that one in four people find a new job straight away, within a month of redundancy, but that the same number are still looking for a job or have entered early retirement over a year later. Half of those who have experienced redundancy say it is important not to just take the first job you are offered. You will need to have a clear resolve if you are to be that strong!

> *'I can give you a six-word formula for success: "Think things through then follow through".'*
> EDDIE RICKENBACKER, EARLY 20TH CENTURY MOTOR RACER AND FIGHTER PILOT

You want to achieve great things in your life and so you need a vision too. If you can create a strong, compelling vision of yourself in a new job role, you can begin to make it happen. You will have a clarity of focus. Stephen Covey picked this out as being one of the seven habits of highly effective people. They 'begin with the end in mind'. With that focus comes determination to succeed. Be focused on a clear goal and you will be more successful at attaining it.

38 WRITE A BOOK

They say everybody has a good book inside them. What's yours?

You might look on this time in your life as a career break. Perhaps you would have been going on a sabbatical if we'd been living in more buoyant economic times and your employer had been amenable to the idea.

If you're honest with yourself, you've still got a wide store of ambitions to fulfil and one of them is writing a book, isn't it? If so, you're not alone – you share that ambition with one in five of the British public, according to a survey by One Life Live. Now you have the time to do it. The hardest task is getting started, so start today. Perhaps you have the idea for a novel or a children's book? Or a non-fiction book based on your personal experiences? Maybe you could write a book about your hobby or personal passion: anything from travel to cookery, from classic cars to gardening.

Don't run away with the idea of being a professional author, at least not yet. Very few people earn enough from writing to be a full-time professional. However, that's not to say you can't earn a little money from being a part-time author. Think also about offering to write articles on a freelance basis for trade magazines and other publications that are generally seeking authors. That will get you started and allow you to demonstrate to others what you can do.

What this also gives you is a new anchor for conversation at your next job interview: your answer to the question of how you have been spending your time since you were made redundant is now filled with something positive to speak about. 'I have always planned to write a book, now for the first time in my life I've had the time to do it.' Writing a book is an active experience. You'll be using your mind to think things through. You'll be carrying out your research: at your local library, using the Internet or talking to different people.

Sue Donnelly made a dramatic change of career from travel agent to professional image coach. As a result of her work as an image coach, she was asked to contribute articles to a variety of women's magazines. The highlight of this time was writing the regular style column for *Health Plus* magazine and then being invited to be an expert speaker on this subject at The Vitality Show. All of this activity culminated in Sue becoming a published author with several books to her name, including *Heading South?*, *80/20 Makeover* and *Feel Fab at Fifty*.

'21% of Britons dream of writing a book – are you one of them?'
'DREAMS OF A BETTER LIFE' SURVEY, ONE LIFE LIVE, 2006

Here's how readily things happened for Sue. What's important to note is how she followed her passion and instincts, with one step leading inexorably to another, culminating in her becoming a published author and coach. 'After attending a training course run by a personal image coach, I realised that this was what I wanted to do with my life. I just knew it! I'd always known I had an eye for colour and had some flair for design. But I hadn't put two and two together before and realised I could make a living as a style consultant.

'I initially went on a series of courses to build my skills as a professional image coach. After one course I stayed behind at the end to thank the trainer. She said she was really impressed with me, she knew I'd make it, and wanted to introduce me to her publisher. I met them and they liked me and my ideas. Over the four years which have followed, I've averaged a book a year. My advice to anyone who wants to write a book is write about your passion and make it happen!'

You may feel you'd like to be a writer but need some training before you can start in this new direction. There are many organisations offering this kind of training. The Open University, for instance, offers short courses to get you started on writing fiction, poetry and plays. These can take as little as twelve weeks. Organisations such as The Writers Bureau offer home study courses to get you started as a published writer. This definition of 'writer' includes writing articles for newspapers and magazines as well as books.

Richard Oldale was made redundant from his job drafting wills for a firm of solicitors. He decided to pursue a career as a writer so took a correspondence course with The Writers Bureau. Richard says, 'I found it very useful. It's a comprehensive course covering journalism, short stories and novels, plus writing for radio and TV. You can do the course in your own time and you get feedback on your writing from professional writers.' Nowadays Richard does a lot of writing for online magazines on subjects as varied as travel, football and music. 'There definitely seem to be more opportunities to write for online magazines than for physical magazines,' says Richard. 'I started off working on an unpaid basis until I had a proven record to show other editors and win paid work. Next I want to turn my hand to writing for TV!'

Why not choose to combine a short break with a residential study course? You can recharge your batteries, make new contacts and develop your writing skills all at once. Why not offer to write an article for the trade magazine for your industry? It'll help raise your profile. Trade magazines

> *'Becoming an author means that others appreciate you are an **author**-ity on your subject. Having books in print allows me to pursue my passion and talk to a global audience. I also love writing. So what could be better than that?'*
>
> SUE DONNELLY, AUTHOR OF PERSONAL IMAGE BOOKS INCLUDING *FEEL FAB AT FIFTY*

often welcome freelance contributions. You might progress from writing articles on a subject to writing a book on that subject.

If you have expertise in a particular area, there's probably a good book in you.

If your profession involves imparting knowledge, there's probably a good book in you.

If you are creative and imaginative in nature, there's probably a good book in you.

If you enjoy reading books yourself, there's probably a good book in you.

Why not use some of the time you now have to write it?

39 SET YOUR FINANCES IN ORDER

First base now is financial survival. You need to take charge of your financial situation. Review all your outgoings and reduce them wherever you can. Make sure you know how long your redundancy money will last.

If income is in short supply, you need to make your money stretch further. If you've been fortunate enough to receive a redundancy payment, your aim should be to make it last as long as possible. Spend at least some of it on things that will benefit you significantly, not just on day-to-day living expenses.

Start by reviewing all your regular monthly outgoings. If you haven't already done so, make a list of all your regular payments each month: your mortgage or rent, telephone and mobile phone, satellite and cable TV, gas and electricity, all of your insurance payments, credit card and loan repayments, and any other regular bills. Now that you have time on your hands, take up the challenge of reducing as many of these bills as possible. Economic times are tough and there are good deals to be had by shopping around. You've known for some time you can find a better deal on your motor and household insurance, haven't you? What about a better deal on your energy bills and your credit card? You've always put it off because of the hassle, because you didn't have the time. Well, now you have time, it's time to throw yourself into this challenge and make some savings!

Check out the renewal date on your insurance policies, but start to shop around now, so you are ready to make that switch when the time comes.

Comparison websites like Gocompare and MoneySavingExpert will help you find the best deals. You might also challenge a local insurance broker to find you a better deal. You'll probably find them only to happy to help.

Change your weekly shopping habits too. Consider switching your supermarket. Shop around for larger items and buy online or in bulk where it is more economical to do so. Consider revising your shopping list. Drop some of the more expensive and indulgent items that you really don't need. Try to find the cheapest place to fill your car with petrol. Regard it as a challenge and try to have some fun in finding the best deals.

'Almost everyone who has been made redundant agrees that it is (in principle) good advice to cut your outgoings and live strictly within your means. But only one person in six actually takes any action to reduce their financial outgoings.'
REDUNDANCY TRANSFORMATIONS STUDY, ALTERNATIVE FUTURES, 2009

Set yourself an overall financial target. This might be to reduce your monthly household bills by £200, for instance. By shopping around and making a series of savings in different places, you might find this is actually easier than you think! Obviously, saving £200 each month in this way has the same financial impact on your household as you going out and earning an extra £200 through freelance work. Yet it is surprising that most people who've been made redundant don't take any action to reduce their financial outgoings.

After achieving this saving, you can feel really good about yourself. You've helped tidy up your life and have brought your finances under control.

This is a good time to take stock of what you own. Look through the things that fill your garage and loft space, and crowd every cupboard. Ask yourself two questions. What items are you in love with? What items are useful? Everything else is clutter and you can spring-clean your life by getting rid of them. If you can't sell items on eBay or through a small ad in your local newspaper, then give them away to a charity shop or visit your local recycling centre. Regard any money you raise from decluttering your life as a bonus. Feel good about yourself for having done it.

According to the Redundancy Transformations Study by Alternative Futures, most people who experience redundancy don't speak to their mortgage provider at all. Two out of every three people with a mortgage do not speak to their bank or building society about the fact that they have lost their jobs. Why not? Many seem to believe that their mortgage provider won't be able to help or won't want to help. Many more, rightly or wrongly, imagine that they are sufficiently financially secure not to need to speak to them. In practice, mortgage providers will always want customers to talk to them at the earliest moment and will often be able to help.

'Money is a terrible master but an excellent servant.'
P.T. BARNUM

According to NatWest, which is building a reputation for itself as 'the helpful bank', it is always best to speak to your mortgage provider as soon as you are made redundant or experience any form of financial hardship. As Chris Lewis from NatWest explains: 'Speaking to your mortgage provider at an early stage allows maximum opportunity for them to work with you and help you through your financial difficulty. It allows time to explain the different ways in which help can be provided; for example, you might find depending on the kind of mortgage you have that your lender is able to offer a period of reduced mortgage payments or even a repayment holiday.'

You will only find this out if you have the courage to pick up the phone and speak to your bank.

Last but not least, you need to have conversations about your entitlements to state benefits. You will want to make an early appointment at your local Jobcentre to ask about Jobseeker's Allowance. Information is also available via the Jobcentre Plus website. If you qualify, you may find your National Insurance contributions continue to be paid and you qualify for free prescriptions and dental care, for instance. Don't assume that because you have some savings or received a redundancy payment you automatically won't qualify. You have paid your tax and National Insurance into the system for many years – now make sure you take your entitlements and draw any support that is on offer. The regulations regarding entitlements are changing all the time so you need to check the latest rules.

Just don't allow yourself to veto this as a course of action because of outdated knowledge or pride!

40 OBTAIN A GRANT OR FUNDING

You may have just received a redundancy payment, but your aim is to invest that money. If you spend it, you want to spend it on making things happen for yourself.

The way forward may involve seeking an additional grant or funding from elsewhere. Be open to this thought because additional funding could make a big difference to what you can do.

If you've decided to start your own business, using your life savings or your redundancy payment to help you, the last thing on your mind could be securing additional sources of funding. Yet it is as near certain as anything can be that in business, cash flow will at some point become a problem. This is particularly the case when trading in a difficult economic climate. At some point a customer will owe you money and so you will struggle to make payments that you owe to someone else. It's a difficult but unfortunately very common situation.

Career Development Loans are interest-free loans, currently of up to £8000. These loans can be obtained for a wide variety of approved retraining courses. If you need to retrain, consider whether a Career Development Loan might help.

The moves you make at the beginning to set up alternative sources of funding for your business could be vital.

When starting up a new business, one of the first places to go for help and assistance is Business Link, the government-funded agency that exists to help new business start-ups and growing businesses. You can attend free workshops and seminars, and access a wealth of advice. All services are generally free. They can tell you about any available grants. Business Link compiles a Grants and Support Directory: a database of grants and support services from central and local government, and from private organisations. Grant opportunities are changing all the time, so make sure you are up-to-date with the current opportunities. Securing a grant could give your business a major boost from the outset.

Is there anyone among your family and friends who would be interested in helping you to fund your business proposition? They might be much more understanding of temporary business difficulties than an external investor would be.

Another place to start is a conversation with your bank. Early discussions with your bank about cash flow forecasts within the business will help you reach the right decisions at the start. You need to clarify your overdraft limit and discuss possible future needs for bank loans. It is much better to have these discussions at the beginning, rather than later on down the track, so that as a business you know exactly what your financial 'wriggle room' is.

You may find that if you are buying a franchise, rather than starting your own business, that banks are much more amenable. This is because the bank views you as a safer bet. You are operating a business under an established brand, with a proven business model and with back-up and support if you encounter trading difficulties. You will also have far less trouble providing the bank with plausible turnover and profit projections, since the franchisor will be able to supply you with this kind of data based on typical franchisee experiences.

Private sources of funding can be explored too. Rather than seek out those experienced individuals who are sometimes dubbed 'angel investors' or 'business angels' – successful businesspeople who invest in businesses they think will make good investments – you may be better advised to start looking a little closer to home. Is there anyone among your family and friends who would be interested in helping you to fund your business proposition? Clearly they might do so in the hope and expectation of future reward, but they might also be much more understanding of temporary business difficulties than an outside investor would be. They could loan money to you as an individual that you offer to pay back with interest at a (flexible) future time. Or perhaps you have friends who are themselves self-employed? Perhaps you could reach some flexible arrangement to enable them to loan you money if you encounter difficulties when their business is doing well, and vice versa?

Or perhaps rather than starting your own business, you are simply looking to retrain? Some training courses that you see advertised may be fully funded if you meet certain criteria. Don't rush to pay the full fee for any training without first enquiring if there is funding available for those who are jobseekers.

Career Development Loans are interest-free loans, currently of up to £8000. These loans can be obtained for a wide variety of approved retraining courses. They may even cover some living expenses during your period of retraining. You can find more information about these loans from Directgov or through banks such as Barclays, RBS or the Co-operative Bank.

Whatever you decide to do, funding it is going to be important, particularly in a challenging economic climate. You may not want to seek outside financial assistance, but obtaining the right kind of funding and the right time could be crucial. Speak to those who might help you, at the earliest possible moment.

41 CREATE A NEW ROUTINE

To overcome redundancy, you first need to get through this tricky transitional time. You've lost not only your job, but also the structure to your day.

To keep going and begin to build, you will need to establish a new routine for yourself.

The daily grind. You used to complain about it, didn't you? Getting up at 6.30 a.m., showering, breakfasting and getting out of the house by 7.30 a.m.? Then the commute to work. A day of meetings and other activities before finishing work and returning home. But what that brief daily snapshot shows is the extent to which your work fashioned the whole structure of your day.

> 'The only place where success comes before work is in the dictionary.'
> VIDAL SASSOON

Now you feel a sense of loss, not just of your job but of the whole structure to your days. Perhaps you have been redundant for a month or two and feel you have begun to drift? Your days have begun to seem aimless?

If so, you need to act now to impose a new routine. This gives your days a predictability and also provides you with a focus. It ensures your new work – the task of seeking work – gets done. You will achieve more if you impose a routine with time limits upon yourself. It really isn't hard to plan it. What is more difficult is keeping yourself to the new routine once you've decided upon it. You will need every ounce of self-discipline that you possess.

Some people also find it helpful to create an office or work-zone within their home. If you haven't already done so, take command of the study and create a filing system for your career reappraisal, job searching and job applications. Speak to your partner, if appropriate, and reserve use of the home computer and telephone for specific times of the day.

Here's a suggestion for a new routine, with my comments on why each suggestion is a good one.

- **7.30 a.m. Wake, shower, breakfast.** It's important to make a reasonably early start. Too much sleep leads to lethargy and you need to keep your energy levels up at this time!
- **8.30 a.m. Early morning walk or other exercise such as swimming or cycling.** Give yourself exercise to keep energy levels up and provide some space to think. Fresh air improves the quality of your thinking.
- **9.30 a.m. Check emails, make phone calls to friends/contacts.** Networking is one of the key ways to get a new job – you need to dedicate time for this every day. It's easy to be cynical about networking, but those who've been made redundant before know just how important it is.
- **10.30 a.m. Prepare job applications and visit job search websites.** Active work to get your next job. What new opportunities can you find or craft today?
- **12.30 p.m. Networking lunch.** This might be with your support group or with former colleagues and contacts who you've arranged to catch up with.
- **2.30 p.m. Household tasks and/or voluntary work/self-development time.** Make progress in other parts of your life, do good turns for other people. Improve your skills or knowledge through some

self-development activity: PC training, reading a business book or something similar.

- **4.00 p.m. Research companies you are interested in joining and make speculative approaches (via contacts there if you have them).** Homework to understand the opportunities out there and try to find a way to introduce yourself to the companies that look most promising. Is there a temporary position you could fulfil or a freelance opportunity that might lead to a permanent job?

- **6.00 p.m. End of working day.** Social or family time – you should have plenty to talk about with your family and friends.

You will want to fashion your own daily routine: one that takes into account your own preferences (what's your best time of day?) and family commitments. Having created a routine, you need to show the self-discipline to stick to it.

42 CHOOSE AN ALTERNATIVE LIFESTYLE

What are the fixed points in your life, the points that you are absolutely unwilling to change? If everything else is fluid, there may be more possibilities for you than you think. An alternative lifestyle may beckon.

Identifying the fixed points in your life is a useful aid to thinking about your future.

So what is absolutely fixed for you: location, salary requirements, working hours? And what is flexible for you: industry, status, perks, whether it is home or office-based work, whether you are a permanent employee or freelancer?

It is helpful to challenge the items you consider to be fixed. Some will be more flexible than you might think! If you say your regional location, your salary requirements and your working hours are fixed, then ask yourself these three questions:

- Under what circumstances is it conceivable that I might move home for a job?
- Under what circumstances could I accept a lower basic rate of pay?
- Under what circumstances could I consider working different (longer or shorter) working hours?

Push back at the fixed points in your thinking to see if they are truly fixed or actually flexible. This is a lateral thinking technique known as provocation. The fixed points in our thinking prevent creativity. For instance, if you are a motor car designer and your view of a motor car is fixed – it must have four wheels, a windscreen with windscreen wipers, a steering wheel, an engine in the front – you will never be the person who designs the car of the future.

In practice, the fixed points in our thinking are generally of our own making. They are mental constructs. Perhaps they should only remain fixed, when thinking about future possibilities, if they are vital for our value system – if they are linked to the things we really believe in and are committed to in our lives.

> *'There is only one success – to be able to spend your life in your own way.'*
> CHRISTOPHER MORLEY

If you are only willing to move some of the fixed points in your thinking, it may open up some radical new possibilities for you. It may even open up an alternative lifestyle. Here are just a few thoughts to demonstrate how flexible thinking might open up opportunities for you:

- **Prepared to move?** Now you can scour the country for vacancies, not just your own patch. You can move to where the work is, even if this is abroad. Or consider working from one location for part of the working week and another location for the rest of the time.

- **Prepared to work for less income?** Now you can consider performance-related pay deals, being rewarded by commission not fixed salary. Consider alternative jobs that pay less but are more rewarding in other ways. Consider a portfolio career, where you might run one part-time job in conjunction with freelance activities, for instance. Consider downsizing, moving to less expensive accommodation and reducing your income needs from your employment accordingly.

- **Prepared to adapt your working hours?** Increasingly, employers may be demanding a more flexible workforce. There are many trade-offs to be made here and different directions in which this thinking might take us. If you accept flexible working arrangements, you might have to work for less pay but be more productive as an employee.

Alternatively, if you are willing to offer to work evenings and weekends, this might make you appear a more attractive candidate. The working hours you consider may be dictated by the practicalities of your life with your partner and your existing childcare arrangements. However, your partner's working hours may not be absolutely fixed and alternative childcare arrangements might be considered. Perhaps you are being too fixed in your thinking right now and ruling out jobs requiring alternative working hours? It's important to talk this through with your partner.

- **Prepared to consider self-employment or working from home?** Perhaps a new life as a freelancer is beckoning you? You might start your own business, working from home to begin with. Or you might take on a job with longer hours, so long as you are able to carry out some of that work from home.

- **Prepared to consider something completely different?** Retraining for a new career may take time, commitment and money, but retraining might also change significantly the way a future employer views you. Perhaps it is time to switch from the private to public sector or vice versa? You might choose a major alternative such as emigration. You might take a career break to pursue a passion or make some other significant change to your lifestyle.

So be as flexible as possible in your thinking. Your current lifestyle could change, if you allow it to. An alternative lifestyle may suit you better. Perhaps it's time to work on your own terms?

ALTERNATIVE LIFESTYLES – CASE STUDY

Here's just one example. Matthew Theobald was made redundant from his job as Head of Service and Support Processes with a global pharmaceuticals company. Rather than go back into corporate life, after receiving coaching support from Penna he set up his own company, Three Circles Consulting, to help clients dramatically increase their success rate. 'I realised I didn't want to go back into corporate life and spend all my time travelling internationally, spending time away from my family,' says Matthew. 'I had a young daughter at the time and wanted to see her growing up. So I set up my own business.

'Now I look back and wish I'd done it earlier! My lifestyle has changed a lot – and for the better. I see more of my family. And I've replaced the support network which I had through my job with a professional network I've built up myself – people who I know and like and who I can rely on. I invest time in adding value to these relationships, sharing knowledge with them, building strategic partnerships not just ringing up to say "How are you?".'

43 GO BACK TO SCHOOL OR UNIVERSITY

How can you develop yourself and make yourself more employable? For some, being made redundant can prompt momentous change in their lives.

Going back to school or university might be hugely beneficial. Academic qualifications may lead you into a better career. You could go to university for the first time, as a mature student, and gain the degree that will propel you into a new job.

> *'The man who is too old to learn was probably always too old to learn.'*
> CARYL HASKINS, SCIENTIST

In these days of students paying their way it won't be a cheap option, but perhaps your redundancy cheque is big enough to allow you to consider it? And with a university course you will also get all of the benefits of a university lifestyle: friends, social life, arts and culture. Maybe there are worse things to do with the next three years!

Or you might effectively 'go back to school' and do the A levels or GCSEs you never completed? Perhaps you rebelled in your teenage years against the constraints of school and never did get the qualifications you were capable of? Maybe that has affected your confidence and prevented you from reaching the level at work that you deserve? It could be time to put things right! That doesn't mean going back to a 'school' setting: you might choose to study at a College of Further Education, via evening classes or by distance learning.

Perhaps you just want to fulfil a lifelong ambition by studying a subject that is of great interest to you, something that has always been a passion. Perhaps doing a degree in art will give you the confidence to exhibit your paintings in public? Perhaps doing a drama degree will lead to something more than amateur dramatics? Perhaps a degree in a foreign language could lead to a new life abroad?

'Following redundancy around one person in twenty goes to university or enters a period of academic study.'

REDUNDANCY TRANSFORMATIONS STUDY, ALTERNATIVE FUTURES, 2009

You don't necessarily need to go down the usual routes for academic learning. Your life commitments may prohibit you from moving home or from certain hours of study. If so, don't reject this idea too quickly. There are many distance learning options.

One of the UK's best-kept secrets, for instance, is that The Open University is now Europe's largest university. It offers far more than just degree courses these days. Many of its courses have no entry requirements. Indeed, you may find you are able to claim credits across from your previous studies.

The OU is built around the principles of distance learning and flexible learning. You can study from home but also get tutor support. You may be able to use one of the many study centres that the OU has all over the country – more than 350 at the time of writing. It doesn't need to take years and cost a fortune. There is a range of introductory courses, open to anyone, lasting just twenty weeks and costing just over £100. You might take an introductory course in law, maths, understanding children or health, for instance. Or you might do a short course such as 'Introduction to counselling', 'Start writing fiction' or 'Understanding human nutrition'. Almost half of new OU students receive financial support. The OU is, of course, just one of many different educational options you might follow.

If you've just been made redundant, you may have two things going for you at this moment. You may have time and you may have money (if you just received a redundancy payment from your employer). This time in your life could be the moment to improve your educational qualifications to propel yourself into a new job or pursue a passion.

RETURNING TO LEARNING – A CASE STUDY

Here's Susan Kilby's story. Susan had worked for the same employer for more than twenty years when she took voluntary redundancy. The package was a good one and the redundancy money enabled her to go to university. This was something she had not done when she was younger because she had a young daughter to look after.

History had always been a passion in Susan's life and she threw herself into her degree course. 'Most universities positively welcome mature students,' Susan says. 'They know they will be hard-working: those who have been working in a job for many years already possess a strong work ethic. Universities know that mature students will be personally committed to learning, particularly if they're studying to bring about a career change.

'I've been able to combine my full-time degree course with up to fifteen hours of part-time and freelance work each week. Many other mature students are doing the same. You can get a Student Loan from the government, but that needs to be paid back. I think it's probably better to self-finance via your redundancy money and do part-time work alongside your degree course to help you through.'

For some people, going back to school or university will be the right move to make, right now. It might be the best way to spend the next period in your life. Make sure it is an option you at least consider. You're never too old to learn!

44 LISTEN TO OTHERS WHO'VE BEEN THERE BEFORE

This is a time when advice from family and friends is welcome. The most important advice to listen to, however, is going to come from people who have been there before: those who have experienced redundancy themselves and professionals who regularly advise people on how to bounce back.

Perhaps the most shocking statistic from the Redundancy Transformations Study is that 42% of people don't seek help from *any* external party following their redundancy.

You don't need to take this journey alone. There are many organisations and professionals who can help you bounce back and find or create a new job for yourself. Those you might speak to include outplacement consultancies, career transition specialists, recruitment consultancies, careers advisers, life coaches, personal image coaches, trade unions, Business Link and the Careers Advice Service.

Some people are also reluctant to take the most obvious action of all – to talk to other people they know who have experienced redundancy and seek their advice. They may be too proud to admit to friends and neighbours that they are in this difficult situation.

Experiences of redundancy are so common nowadays that it is foolish to be embarrassed about discussing it. If you do speak to others about your current situation, you will be surprised how many people will have a story about a past redundancy or period of unemployment in their

Don't be too proud to seek the advice of others. Draw on the experiences of those who've been there before.

own lives to share with you. The more people you speak to who have been there before, the more practical advice you will collect. You do not have to learn how to cope with redundancy on your own – you can draw on the previous learning and experience of others.

The Redundancy Transformations Study by Alternative Futures captured the experiences of more than a thousand British people who had experienced redundancy in their lives. Around 60% of them felt their lives were better now than before the redundancy. Those whose lives had been transformed positively outnumbered those whose lives had suffered by a ratio of two to one. Why was this? Well, eight out of ten of those who'd seen their lives improve said that redundancy was the spur for them to make major changes in their lives. Here are just a few of their comments in response to the question 'What do you know now, that you wish you had been told by someone at the time?'.

- 'Don't blame yourself! It gives you a chance to start again with a more profitable company and more opportunities. It also gives you a chance to leave behind any baggage.'
- 'It's the job, not you that had to go. Believe it!'
- 'You need to be positive and believe there is light at the end of the tunnel. I wish I'd had the confidence at the time to go for other jobs which I thought at the time were beyond my reach.'
- 'That this would be the best thing that could ever happen to me! I now realise that though I was one of the first redundancies in my company I definitely had the best deal.'
- 'That I have so much strength within me. Yes, there were shaky times but part of who I am now has come from the experience I have gained from being made redundant. You are capable of far more than you ever give yourself credit for!'

- 'The first practical steps to entitlements, Jobseeker's Allowance, getting your stamp paid – that kind of thing. Jobcentres are soul-destroying places but if you can face your first session armed with a few facts it would be less daunting.'
- 'I think one piece of advice is that you *will* get through this redundancy, although things might be tough for a while.'
- 'That it was going to be a transition period and that it was OK to explore different ideas.'
- 'That these things usually turn out for the best. I spent a lot of time worrying about things I could not influence instead of focusing on the things that I could make happen.'
- 'That my job wasn't the be-all and end-all to life.'
- 'Don't be afraid of making possible life-changing decisions.'
- 'A different set of values and lifestyle can make you see what is really important in life.'
- 'That I should have started my own business years ago with all the experience I had.'
- 'That it was easier than I thought to start up my own business as there is a lot more help out there than I realised.'
- 'To get professional help with your CV.'
- 'Freelancing is the only way to go, really.'
- 'Go to work abroad. I did it later for five years and should have done it years before.'
- 'Keep positive and resister with every agency and talk to anyone else you know in your industry. Take up any temporary work that's going to help with the day-to-day expenses of your home'
- 'Let all your friends and family know what is happening. There's no shame and you never know what opportunities it might generate.'

45 WORK ABROAD

Free movement of labour within the European Union applies to you as well! You now have the right to move to take up a job anywhere in the EU.

There are many job opportunities in other countries. Someone, somewhere is looking for a person with just your mix of skills and experience. Are you prepared to seek them out and move to take that job?

'If you are willing to move out into the world, you might find a world of opportunities waiting for you! We see 20,000 Britons every year who visit the One Life Live show and then change their lives dramatically – by moving abroad to work or retire, buying properties abroad or volunteering for work overseas.'

HELEN MARRIOTT, ONE LIFE LIVE

If you don't have commitments that absolutely prevent you from moving abroad, seeking a job overseas could be a real option for you. Moving abroad need not be permanent. It could just be a short-term move, for a year or two to fulfil a contract. Consider this: it might also prove to be the experience of your life!

In a survey for the first One Life Live exhibition in 2006, emigrating to start a new life abroad was shown to be the top dream of the British public. Half of us dream of emigrating (given the chance), with Australia, New Zealand, Spain, the USA and Canada being our top choices of where to go. Britain has its fair share of *Shirley Valentine* 'wannabes' too, with one in ten of us dreaming of emigrating to the Greek islands.

The second most common dream of the British public is to travel the world. Naturally these two top dreams can go hand in hand: if you move abroad to work, you can experience a new country. You can also travel within that country and beyond to some of its neighbours. If you base yourself in the UK, your usual choice of holiday destinations may be within Western Europe. If you base yourself in Australia, your holidays might well be to Bali, Thailand or China. If you base yourself in the USA, you might readily holiday in Mexico, Canada or Hawaii.

'86% of Britons dream of a new and different life and 51% dream of emigrating.'

'DREAMS OF A BETTER LIFE' SURVEY, ONE LIFE LIVE, 2006

However, the reality of working abroad may be more *Auf Wiedersehen, Pet* than *Shirley Valentine*. If you're involved in a practical trade (such as a carpenter, painter, plumber or builder), or even if you work in medicine or education, you may find more similarities in practice than differences. Don't give yourself false expectations that it's all going to be different or glamorous.

There are always going to be some skills that are in demand worldwide. One opportunity for us is the massive demand that exists worldwide to learn English. Could you teach English as a foreign language? You might attend a TEFL (Teaching English as a Foreign Language) course in the UK and learn how to teach English abroad.

Could you work in one of the main expat industries? Industries such as engineering, construction, oil and gas have always employed large numbers of British expats, frequently on a contract basis. Could you work within the travel industry, based abroad but helping to serve the needs of British international travellers? As well as jobs in the holiday trade, hotels and restaurants there are specialist jobs serving particular traveller needs. If you have prior experience of living in a particular country, you might help British business people to relocate there, rent property there and source schools for their children.

Could you take your professional skill and import it into a country that you know has a shortage of that skill? Clearly teachers and health professionals are always in demand worldwide, and are particularly needed in the developing world. Could you train or coach English-speaking managers who are based abroad?

Perhaps you would like to volunteer to do charitable work overseas through an organisation like VSO (Voluntary Service Overseas)? Rob Breare is the founder of Skills Venture, an organisation that matches British business people with entrepreneurs in Kenya. Business people with more than five years' commercial experience are matched with Kenyan businesses that need advice. Rob says: 'Our volunteers stay anything from a few days up to six months, but they can all make a difference. The experience will make a positive difference on the life of the volunteer too! As an example of what's possible, one Kenyan yoghurt-maker expanded with help from our volunteers and grew from being a one-man business to one which is on its way to supporting 200 local farmers and employing nearly twenty people.'

Take time to think seriously about whether working abroad is a real possibility for you. Your existing commitments may be renegotiated or creative ways found to honour them. If you seriously consider emigrating, make sure you research it well. Talk to organisations that have experience of helping Britons to emigrate before you make a decision. Speak to ordinary people who have lived in that country before. Increase your knowledge of the reality of life in another country. The reality may be different from your imagination!

46 FIND INSPIRATION

Feed your motivation. Look for inspiration by visiting inspirational events, reading books that will be uplifting and listening to CDs by motivational speakers.

Stephen Covey, Susan Jeffers, Zig Ziglar, Anthony Robbins, Edward de Bono and many others are people who can help you out of the place you find yourself right now.

> *'You can have everything in life if you will just help others to get what they want.'*
> ZIG ZIGLAR , MOTIVATIONAL AUTHOR AND SPEAKER

They are inspirational authors and speakers who can help you look at your life and the challenges facing you in a different way. There is an array of self-help literature out there to help sustain you through the days ahead. If you make a point of reading it, or listening to it, some of it will strike a chord within you. That's almost certain. It is practically impossible to read or listen to these individuals without feeling energised and motivated by some of their words.

When I set up my own business eight years ago, I found the following authors and their works particularly uplifting. I used the evenings to read books and the car journeys to listen to tapes, to help me absorb some of the lessons. I can thoroughly recommend each of the following:

- **Stephen Covey's *The Seven Habits of Highly Effective People.*** If you come out of reading this book adopting even one of the seven habits, you'll be a better person. Take for example Habit Number 1, 'Be proactive'. If you can make things happen, by networking and making contacts, by doing favours for other people that they will repay, then you can create opportunities for yourself. Or Habit Number 2, 'Begin with the end in mind': if you can create a clear vision of the job you want or the business you want to create, you're well on the way to getting there.

- **Susan Jeffers'** *Feel the Fear and Do It Anyway.* This book underlines the thought that brave people aren't those without any fear – they are people who don't allow their fear to stop them from doing what they want to do. You might be afraid now, about retraining and taking your career in a completely new direction, about your financial situation, or about whether or not you've got what it takes to be successfully self-employed. But don't let the fear stop you. Feel the fear and do it anyway.

- **Zig Ziglar's** *Five Steps to Successful Selling* **(audiobook).** For those who are starting up their own business, sales skills are going to be very important. You may be technically proficient and so may be able to follow the processes and do the technical work to a very high standard, but how will you make the sale in the first place? How do you prospect for sales and convince someone else to buy from you? Equally, if you are going for job interviews, you need to learn to 'sell yourself' persuasively at interview. Zig Ziglar is someone who helps you see the simple principles of selling and underlines how you can get what you want in life by helping other people get what they want. Stephen Covey makes a similar kind of point: Habit Number 6 of highly effective people is 'Seek first to understand, then to be understood'. One of the principles of successful salesmanship is to get the customer to talk about their needs and then explain how what you are offering will help answer their needs.

Find some authors whose words will motivate you.

Use spare moments each day to read self-help literature and practical books. They will help you to take your next steps and set you on the stairs that lead upwards. Seek out books on effective networking, interview technique, running your own business, life coaching, assertiveness, career development or whatever areas you feel you are most in need of support.

'Undoubtedly, we become what we envisage.'
CLAUDE M. BRISTOL, SELF-HELP AUTHOR

Get out to visit events that will give you ideas and motivate you. There are many free or low-cost exhibitions and seminars that can provide a fund of ideas. One event, which is held in London every spring, is the One Life Live exhibition. Here, under one roof, you will find organisations that can help you with major life changes such as starting your own business, volunteering, retraining for a new career, emigration and international travel. The One Life Live exhibition also runs a series of workshops with motivational speakers in parallel with the exhibition itself. Look out for this kind of event and other events that are close to you. You will emerge energised and enthused.

At this time in your life you need to surround yourself with positive influences. You need to listen to positive voices, people who believe things can happen rather than those who wallow in their own pessimism and pour cold water on the hopes of others. Seek out the company of people you know and admire. If there is a former colleague or old friend you admire but you've lost touch with, try to find out where they are now and meet up again. If you are considering launching your own business, find someone to speak to who has done it themselves and is successful. If you are thinking of moving into a different career, find someone who is successful in that career to speak to. Seek out people you admire, tell them how much you admire them, and ask them the secret of their success. You are likely to find them willing to share their experiences with you.

Be inspired!

47 ENROL WITH A COACH

You may be able to do it alone, but you'll reach your goal more easily and quickly if you get help. You'll be more successful if you can have a clear focus on the right direction for you and make the right moves.

Why enrol with a coach? It's not compulsory. Many will make their way without a formal coach to help them.

However, a coach can help you to know your own mind, identify your strengths and build on them, and identify your weaknesses and reduce them. A coach can help you to find the right way forward.

There are many different types of coaches around, each of whom might help you in different ways.

A **life coach** (or personal coach) can help with major life decisions, involving the personal aspects of your life to a greater extent than the professional. They might help you with feelings of rejection linked to divorce, relationship breakdown or redundancy, or with addressing limiting beliefs about yourself that might be holding you back in your working life as well as your personal life.

A different career direction could flow out of this assistance. You might feel you'd like to be a teacher but are nervous about speaking in front of groups. Or you may feel you lack the assertiveness to deal with class discipline. Here, personal factors are holding you back and restricting your career choices. Or you might be considering going into business for yourself, working from home, but be unsure how this would affect the relationship you have with your partner. Once again, the career decision and the life issue go hand in hand. Talking things through with a life coach could help you make the right decision.

A **professional image coach** will help you with the way you dress and help you discover what your clothes say about you. You may find that coaching sessions that focus on personal image can provide a major boost to your self-confidence. They might make the difference between shining in that interview and being overlooked for the job.

A **business coach** can help you with the challenges of starting up a new business. Such a coach might help with issues such as choosing the right legal status for your business (sole trader, limited company, partnership or limited liability partnership), or help you to think through your business strategy.

In the early days of running your own business you will probably feel uncertain about many things. You might be concerned about dealing with red tape. Should you register for VAT? What accounts records do you need to retain? You may be faced by the common business challenges of either having too few customers (and wondering how to get more), or feeling drowned in orders (and wondering how you will ever fulfil them all). A business coach can be an expert at your shoulder during these challenging early days.

'People who experience redundancy often find a coach can help them clarify their goals and find the motivation to take action, especially during a time in which they are often re-evaluating their life and future career direction. We find many people bouncing back from redundancy by retraining with us with a view to becoming a professional coach or simply to add coaching to their current skill set. They come to us because we're the market leader in coach training throughout Europe and offer a free introductory event so that they can see what we can do for them.'

KRIS ROBERTSON, DIRECTOR, THE COACHING ACADEMY

An **executive coach** can help you with your personal leadership style and deal with some of your managerial qualities that may need some attention. It may be that you feel the way you communicate decisions or monitor and motivate your staff could be improved upon – an executive coach can help you work on aspects of your performance and help make you into a better manager.

How would you answer the question, at a job interview, about your greatest weaknesses as a manager? You might answer by saying 'I'm aware that I've sometimes been reluctant to delegate as readily as I might, so that's something I've been concentrating on in my weekly executive coaching sessions. I've been funding these myself for the last few months out of my redundancy payment because I want to develop into the best manager I possibly can be.' Does that sound like a good answer to be able to give?

How do you find a coach? Start by asking friends and former colleagues whether they know anyone they can recommend. If this doesn't help, approach professional bodies that represent different types of coaches. These include the Association for Coaching and the Federation of Image Consultants. Or you can make use of the matchmaking service offered by the Coaching Academy, the UK's largest training organisation for coaches. If you register your details on the Coaching Academy's website, they'll try to put you in touch with a coach who meets your needs.

You'll find no lack of coaches out there. The key is to choose a coach who you trust, who can help you in the particular area you need to make progress. Make sure you will get on well at a personal level with your coach. With help, you'll go far!

48 SET UP YOUR OWN SUPPORT GROUP

To get through this and emerge a stronger person, you are going to need support. You need personal contact, encouragement and practical help. If there isn't a ready-made group out there for you to join, you need to set up your own support group.

To admit you need support at all can be a big step for some people. We're sometimes too proud to ask for help, to show people that we have a need. If you don't want to make life harder for yourself, then it's time to ditch that pride right now. Pride could be holding you back from helping others as well as stopping you from attracting help to yourself.

You need to fill your days with constructive activity, networking and the search for a new job or the beginnings of a period of self-employment. One regular activity you should consider is a weekly meeting with your support group.

There may be an obvious support group out there for you to join or create:

- A formal group that already exists for other reasons, such as Rotary, Lions Club or Toastmasters.
- A group of friends who you already meet occasionally and could meet more regularly.
- Friends from school or university who have spare time and would welcome a regular get-together.
- Other jobseekers who live in your town.

- Former colleagues who have been made redundant at the same time as you who would be amenable to forming an 'Exes club'.

Thinking about former colleagues from all of your previous employers (not just your last one) who you liked could be a good place to start. Online services like LinkedIn help you to hook up with them again. LinkedIn is a kind of Friends Reunited for business, helping you to get back in contact with people who used to work at the same workplace as you and you'd lost touch with. Plaxo is another good website that helps you to connect with previous colleagues.

At this time in your life, you need support and encouragement more than ever. Don't be too proud to seek support!

What you need to form, though, is more than just an online group. It is a physical support group: people you can meet up with, share food and drink with, and who you can discuss your situation with – people who you will look forward to meeting who can lift your spirits. Once you've identified who might belong to this group, think about a venue, a regular meeting time and perhaps another activity for the meeting that would help make it enjoyable and worthwhile. Depending on who is in your group, and how well you know them, any of the following kinds of invitations might be appropriate:

- 'Let's meet over lunch on Wednesdays to catch up and see if we can help one another.'
- 'Let's meet up over a cup of tea on Sunday to check how everyone's doing and organise some voluntary activities for the next week.'
- 'Let's go bowling on Friday nights and have a quick drink and catch up afterwards.'
- 'Let's meet at my house on Tuesday afternoons for coffee to check we're each keeping to our agreed weekly goals and swap contacts.'

If it is your support group, you need to take the lead in setting it up and making sure it happens. Ensure there is good camaraderie in the group: you only want to invite people who will get along together. Make sure you fill your group with positive people, encouraging voices, people who want to make things happen rather than 'difficulty staters', people who will always try to find a reason why it won't work and can't happen.

Here's some advice from people who've been there before, some of the respondents on the Redundancy Transformations Study carried out by Alternative Futures Research:

- 'I have some amazingly supportive friends. A couple of them are Company Directors themselves and act as mentors for me. Their advice was invaluable, their support and encouragement vital to my success.'
- 'I wanted to avoid people altogether but I forced myself to talk to people who helped me feel more positive and made efforts to avoid people I found negative or depressing.'
- 'Making the most of my contact pool, networking actively with them (including a large group of former employees) proved to be a key ingredient in my success.'
- 'I found the courage to take voluntary redundancy because of a development programme called Toastmasters. You can go along to any UK meeting (guests are always welcome). It is a non-profit making organisation where you are supported and offered support to learn skills such as thinking on your feet, presentation, evaluation, how to give feedback, leadership and so much more. It is a joy to watch people from all walks of life develop and grow in confidence. It's a real confidence-booster for those with low self-esteem.'

You need support at this time, so find yourself a support group.

49 CREATE A PORTFOLIO CAREER

At the moment you're probably thinking about finding a new job. A straight swap – a new job just like your old one, which can take its place.

But the right solution for you could be something completely different, such as two part-time jobs that taken together provide the income you need. Or a part-time role coupled with freelancing activities. Be open to all the possibilities.

The world of work is changing. We once faced up to the challenging thought that there was no longer such a thing as a job for life. Soon we may have to get used to the stranger idea that the old model of employment – mainly full-time, permanent jobs stationed at a fixed workplace – no longer applies, in general. Employers may seek more flexible mobile workforces featuring a different mix of permanent, part-time and predominantly home-based contract staff.

More than twenty years ago the management guru Charles Handy looked at the future of working practices and predicted that in the twenty-first century, more than 50% of jobs would be something other than full-time. He foresaw a growing number of part-time, flexitime, temporary and self-employment options being used. With the impetus to change employment practices provided by a global recession, perhaps we are about to see Charles Handy's vision becoming the reality?

If you used to be a manager in an industry that is suffering from the economic downturn, it may be very hard for you to find a like-for-like swap. It may be very difficult to find another full-time permanent job just like your last one. Funnily enough, it might be easier for you to find two jobs (part-time or short-term) than one.

Your 'Monday to Friday 9 to 5' may be about to become your 'Monday to Wednesday 9 to 5 and Thursday to Friday 12 to 6', only with two different employers. What's wrong with that? Variety is

Two jobs may be better than one – and easier to find.

the spice of life. You may enjoy having a greater variety of work, even if it requires more planning to juggle your family commitments. The two jobs option does not necessarily imply deterioration in your work-life balance. It may mean living on less income, but not necessarily.

Clearly, a portfolio career, where you combine several different jobs at once, has its attractions. Daniel Gilbert, the author of a best-selling book *Stumbling on Happiness*, believes the best way for you to find out what will make you happy is to try it. A portfolio career will give you the chance to try out two or three types of work, all at the same time!

Certain fields such as academia or the arts, lend themselves naturally to portfolio careers. Lecturer plus writer and non-executive director, perhaps? Some industries, such as farming, have been practising portfolio careers for years, although in agriculture they call it 'diversification'. I well remember taking my family on holiday on a farm when my children were young. The attraction of this particular holiday was that the farmer allowed the young children to get involved with feeding the animals at feeding time. Both my son and daughter loved animals. The farmer not only ran his agricultural smallholding, with its farm shop and bed & breakfast, he also worked part-time as a graphic designer.

Here are a few thoughts. One of them might strike a chord with you. Why not try to combine a morning-only part-time job with working as a freelancer in the afternoons or evenings? Why not teach an evening class while working elsewhere in the mornings or afternoons? Why not set up your own sole trader business with the target of earning just half your previous earnings and look for a part-time job or contract job to make up the income gap?

Perhaps you also know enough about certain subjects to teach others about them or write about them, and do this alongside another job? Perhaps a private passion (such as collecting antiques, paintings, jewellery or classic cars) could become the basis for your own part-time small business that you run alongside another job?

Perhaps the question you should be asking yourself right now is what *combination of careers* would bring in sufficient money and also keep you happy?

50 DOWNSHIFT YOUR LIFE

Downshifting your life is not necessarily a step backwards. It can be an acceptance that 'less is more'.

You can leave a house that is expensive to maintain with rooms you don't use or no longer need. Declutter your life. Waste less. Reuse and recycle rather than buy new. It can all add up to greater personal satisfaction.

In a time of static or falling property prices, many of us have probably shelved the dream of downsizing to fund a wealthy retirement. However, it is not just your house that has gone down in value, but others as well. A difference in price between the house you currently live in and the house that would be the

'If a man does not keep pace with his companions, perhaps it is because he hears a different drummer. Let him step to the music he hears.'

HENRY DAVID THOREAU

minimum to meet your needs still exists. If you are able to sell, then downshifting can still make economic sense. You can move to a smaller property, perhaps in a cheaper part of the country, or emigrate to a country where property prices are much lower than in the UK. The cash you set free from making that move can help to fund a different future lifestyle.

That's what George (one of the respondents on the Redundancy Transformations Study) did. As he explains, 'I'd been a senior manager at the company. We lived in a large four-bedroom home and our mortgage was paid up. My family had all grown up and left home, so we sold up, moved to a bungalow and I retrained as a golf coach. I'd been travelling over 100,000 miles in my job and this had been affecting my health – high blood pressure, tiredness and regular small illnesses. This has all stopped now and I'm feeling much more healthy.'

What if you can't sell? At a time when property prices are declining and new mortgages are hard to come by, fewer people are buying and more are renting. The property rental sector may do well in the years ahead. If so, turn yourself into a landlord. Rent out the property you are currently living in, move to a smaller rented property yourself and use the regular income from the house you rent to fund your new, more frugal life.

Turning yourself from owner-occupier into a landlord to fund a new life was the choice that Alex (another of the respondents on the Redundancy Transformations Study) made. 'I travelled to South America after studying for qualifications here in the UK. I spent two years teaching and volunteering in Bolivia while tenants in the UK subsidised my unpaid work out there.'

Don't want to move? Why not make use of the empty space in your home? Rent out that spare room to a lodger and bring in extra income that way.

We make ourselves richer by making our needs fewer.

Now declutter your life.

Take stock of your possessions. Identify those you want to keep and those you can live without. Then sell your unwanted goods on eBay or a boot sale. Or give away the things you no longer need to local charity shops and good causes. Throw out the broken items (which you know you'll never repair) and the junk that is blocking up your garage, loft and cupboards.

If nothing else, giving a spring-clean to your possessions will lift your spirits. You'll feel lighter if you travel through the rest of your life without all this baggage.

Don't worry that you're not keeping up with your neighbours or peer group. Success in life can be whatever you define it to be. With the global economic crisis, some have already dubbed this the New Age of Frugality. Maybe you are just one of the trendsetters, one of the first to embrace a trend for leaner, lighter living?

Perhaps you've been marching all your life to the beat of one drummer and its time to start marching to the beat of another?

51 ENJOY TIME WITH YOUR FAMILY

When you were in work, you wanted more time with your family. Now you have it. It may only be for a short time, so enjoy it. Make the most of living – now.

We all know that in Britain we work hard. Our average working week in 44 hours, longer working hours than almost any other European country.

As a result, the growing demand from employees over the last decade has been for a better work-life balance. According to the National Employee Opinion Survey by Alternative Futures, work-life balance is second only to pay in terms of what's important to employees.

'84% of those who've experienced redundancy say it is important to enjoy the extra time with your family that the situation has given you.'

REDUNDANCY TRANSFORMATIONS STUDY, ALTERNATIVE FUTURES, 2009

Just think about this for a moment. Before you were made redundant, what sort of things were you saying to your family and friends? That you'd love to get home from work earlier, spend some more time with them, but that your workload was unremitting? That you'd love to get away for a weekend away or a holiday but that it would have to wait until later in the year, when things were a little quieter at work? That you'd love to come to see your son or daughter taking part in the school's Sports Day, but it's scheduled for the middle of the working day and you simply can't get away?

Now you have that opportunity. Now you have that priceless commodity – *time*. Don't waste this precious moment by being morose, flat and miserable. Make sure you enjoy each free day now you have it.

If now is not the right time for a weekend away or short holiday with your family, when on earth will be?

If now is not the time for – if you'll forgive the terrible phrase – some 'quality time' with your partner and children, or to get together again with old friends, when will be?

> *'Work is what you do so that some time you won't have to do it any more.'*
>
> ALFRED POLGAR, AUSTRIAN WRITER

If now is not the time to start up a hobby or take an evening class, when will be?

If not now, then never!

Hang on, I hear you say – money is tight. I've got to be completely focused on finding a new job or starting up in business for myself. That's true, but time with your family costs nothing. You'll be more likely to be accepted for a new job if you are refreshed and happy rather than sad and stressed. A weekend away need not break the bank. Life is for living.

This is a time for you to reaffirm what's important in your life. It's a time when you need support from your family but also a time you can give something back to them in return. Don't make spending time with your family an alternative to job-hunting – make it something you do in parallel to it. You'll be a rounder, happier person if you don't make redundancy an excuse to punish your family. Don't inflict punishment on them by being miserable and constantly bemoaning your bad luck.

You make your own luck. As Thomas Jefferson said, 'I am a great believer in luck, and I find the harder I work the more I have of it.' You also have the power to set your own moods. You can choose to start each day being positive or negative, optimistic or pessimistic.

You can make this period into a positive family time. The power to do this is in your hands.

So what will you do today?

52 BELIEVE IN YOURSELF!

You are capable of bouncing back from redundancy. Your life is going to be better in future, not worse. This situation has been a call to action, a challenge to see how you will respond. Everything is possible if first you believe in yourself.

Don't make the mistake of defining your own value as a person in terms of work. As David D. Burns succinctly put it, 'your work is not your worth'. You are far more than that. You are capable of much more.

There is a study of success that is known as NLP: neuro-linguistic programming to give it its full title, though this can sound rather academic and off-putting. NLP was developed in the USA by a maths undergraduate, Richard Bandler, who had an interest in computing and psychology, working with Dr John Grinder, an Associate Professor of linguistics. It was Bandler and Grinder who first proposed trying to replicate the results of another person by modelling their behaviours and methods.

The conclusions they arrived at are far-reaching. Bandler and Grinder proposed that if one person can do something, someone else can learn to do it by emulating their thinking and behaviour. So you (yes, you!), if you really wanted to, could learn to think and behave like a successful entrepreneur, an inspirational teacher or a selfless campaigner for charitable causes – or someone else you greatly admire.

But first you must believe in yourself! If you begin by saying to yourself 'They are much better people than me, I couldn't hope to be as successful as them' or 'I could never do that!' then you never will – that much is certain. If you think you are beaten, you are. However, if you believe in yourself and follow the instruction of Ella Wheeler Wilcox to 'trust in your own untried capacity', you can aim much higher than the level you are at today.

If you are to emulate the success of others, the first thing you need to do is to get closer to them. Try to understand the way they think. Try to understand the way they act. If you want to become a successful entrepreneur like Duncan Bannatyne or Richard Branson, begin by reading their autobiographies. Read press articles about their lives. Research the way they think and the decisions they take. Try to absorb their mindset and follow their lead. Imagine the same for yourself. You may yet become the person you envisage.

> *'Many a man is building for himself in his imagination a bungalow, when he should be building a palace.'*
> FLORENCE SCOVELL SHINN , SELF HELP WRITER

If you can achieve even a fraction of their success, you will be very successful indeed!

Perhaps your definition of success is somewhat different? Perhaps the person you admire most is someone a little closer to home: a relative or an old school-friend who has gone on to achieve success. By 'success', I mean success *in your view*, however you choose to define it. This may or may not involve material success – perhaps they have a lifestyle that you admire, or an alternative outlook or opinions that inspire you.

Your first step should be to believe in yourself: you too could do what they have done. Your second step should be to talk to the person you admire. Tell them how much you admire them and why. Ask them to tell you the story of how they have achieved all the things they have achieved. As they talk, make note of the way they thought at each key moment in their lives and the actions they took. Look particularly closely at how they handled obstacles or setbacks in their lives. Did they ever suffer redundancy or something similar – and if so, what did they do? You should seek to emulate them. How would they react if they were in your shoes right now?

Imitation really is the sincerest form of flattery!

Here's how Anthony Robbins, the successful author and motivational speaker, puts it. 'Often we are caught in a mental trap of seeing enormously successful people and thinking they are where they are because they have some special gift. Yet a closer look shows that the greatest gift that extraordinarily successful people have over the average person is their ability to get themselves to take action.'

'What lies behind us and what lies before us are tiny matters compared to what lies within us.'
RALPH WALDO EMERSON

Redundancy is the fifth most common Pivot Point that people experience in their lives, according to research by Alternative Futures. Along with marriage, divorce, the birth of children and the death of loved ones, redundancy is the other main turning point people commonly experience in their lives. This moment, containing the experience of redundancy, is a time when *your* life might turn around completely.

Remember that two out of every three people whose life is changed by redundancy will actually see their lives transformed *positively*. Resolve to be one of the people for whom life gets better. The same research shows that 86% of those whose lives changed for the better said that redundancy provided the spur for them to make major changes in their lives.

What changes do you want to make in your life?

You can make the changes that are needed but first you must believe in yourself. As Henry Ford once said, 'if you think you can or think you can't, you're probably right'. Your future can be bright. Believe in yourself and start to build it.

APPENDIX: USEFUL CONTACTS

PENNA

Leading outplacement consultancy offering career transition services, executive coaching, interim management and executive recruitment services.

www.penna.com

ONE LIFE

Annual exhibition to help individuals who are looking to make major life changes.

www.onelifelive.co.uk

BUSINESS LINK

Free advice, workshops and seminars for people wanting to start up their own business.

www.businesslink.gov.uk

CAREERS ADVICE SERVICE

Free careers advice and training course search.

www.careersadvice.direct.gov.uk

JOBCENTRE PLUS

Help on getting back to work and advice on benefits/entitlements.

www.jobcentreplus.gov.uk

DIRECTGOV
Website giving information about all government support and services including training and education, career development loans, employment and mortgage debt advice.

www.direct.gov.uk

OVERCOMING REDUNDANCY
New website to help those affected by redundancy.

www.overcoming-redundancy.com

INFINITE IDEAS
Leading publisher of self-help books including the 52 Brilliant Ideas series.

www.infideas.com

BRITISH FRANCHISE ASSOCIATION
Information about franchising.

www.thebfa.org

TIME BANKING
Exchange an hour of your time for an hour of someone else's.

www.timebanking.org

GOCOMPARE
Price comparison website.

www.gocompare.com

MONEYSAVINGEXPERT
Advice on saving money.

www.moneysavingexpert.com

VOLUNTARY SERVICE OVERSEAS

Leading development charity using volunteers to fight poverty in developing countries.

www.vso.org.uk

SKILLS VENTURE

Short assignments for UK business people in Kenya, supporting Kenyan entrepreneurs.

www.skillsventure.com

OTHER HELPFUL BOOKS FROM INFINITE IDEAS

How to get a job in a recession
Harry Freedman·

High impact CVs:
52 brilliant ideas for making your résumé sensational
John Middleton

Knockout interview answers:
52 brilliant ideas to make job hunting a piece of cake
Ken Langdon and Nikki Cartwright

Cultivate a cool career:
52 brilliant ideas for reaching the top
Ken Langdon

Networking: work your contacts to supercharge your career
Nicolas King

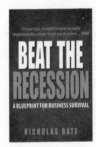

Beat the recession:
a blueprint for business survival
Nicholas Bate

Sort out your money: the only personal finance book
you need to get you through the recession
Ken Langdon and John Middleton

Downshift to the good life:
52 brilliant ideas to scale it down and live it up
Lynn Huggins-Cooper

Be your own best life coach: take charge and live the life you always wanted
Jackee Holder

How to sell and market your way out of this recession and get your business buzzing like never before
Nicholas Bate

INDEX

active, staying 14–16, 17
advice 135–7
Alternative Futures 2, 113, 136, 155
alternative lifestyle 128–30
ambitions 45–6
angel investors 123
Association for Coaching 146
authors 114–17

Bandler, Richard 157
banks 39, 40, 88, 89–90, 94, 120,
    123, 124
Barclays 40, 124
batteries, recharging 47–8
bereavement 4–5
bitterness 29–32
British Franchise Association (BFA)
    95, 167
British and International Franchise
    Exhibition 95
Burns, David D. 157
business angels 123
business coach 145
business contacts 18–19
Business Link 21, 39, 87–8, 89,
    122–3, 135, 166
Business Network International
    (BNI) 21
Business Referral Exchange (BXI) 21

calmness 105–7
Career Anchoring 68
career combinations 150–52
Career Development Loans 36,
    39–40, 124
career guidance 67–70
career transition services 36

Careers Advice Service 36, 65, 68–9,
    135, 166
case studies 6–7, 12–13, 22–3, 37–8,
    43–4, 72–4, 91–2, 131, 134
Chamber of Commerce 21
change 11–13, 27–8, 136
close the book 97–8
clothes 103–4
Co-operative Bank 40, 124
coaches 144–6
Coaching Academy 6, 146
colleagues 18–19, 20
communication 102
community work 24–6
connections 20–23
contingency plans 105–6
Covey, Stephen 141–2
CVs 12, 52–4, 58–9, 82

daily tasks 15
de-cluttering 119–20, 153, 154
Directgov 36, 40, 124, 167
Donnelly, Sue 75–6, 102–3,
    115
downshift 9, 33, 81, 153–4

education 132–4
elevator speech 61–3
email 59, 60
European Union (EU) 138
evening classes 39
excercise 15
executive coach 146
executive search consultants 54

family time 155–6
fear 27–8

Federation of Image Consultants 102, 146
financial paperwork 15–16
financial situation 105, 118–21, 129
financial targets 119
first impressions 103–4
fixed point thinking 128–30
flexible thinking 128–30
focus 111–13
former employers 4–7
four-point schedule 112
franchise 2, 8, 28, 72, 93–6, 123
freedoms 48
freelance 8, 21, 22, 25, 48, 63, 66, 78, 83–5
friends 17–19, 59, 124
Friends Reunited 20, 148
funding sources 122–4

general recruitment consultants 54
Gilbert, Daniel 151
goals 80–82
Gocompare 119, 167
good causes 15
good turns 24–6
grants 122–4
Grinder, Dr John 157

Handy, Charles 83, 150

image 102–4
imitation 157–9
Infinite Ideas 167
inner peace 105–7
inspiration 141–3
insurance 88
insurance policies 118–29
interim positions 78–9
interview technique 108–10
interviews 30, 46, 82, 103–4

Jeffers, Susan 142
Jobcentre 120
Jobcentre Plus 121, 166

Jobseekers' Allowance 120

legal status 89–90
libraries 40–41, 65
life coach 144–5
life review 99–101
limited company 89–92
limited liability partnership 90
LinkedIn 20, 59, 148
lists 15
looking for work 80–82

MoneySavingExpert 119, 167
mortgage providers 120
motivation 141–3
moving abroad 138–40
moving home 129, 154
moving on 4–5

National Employer Opinion Survey 155
NatWest 89–90, 120
negative attitude 29–32, 97–8
networking 17–19, 20, 40, 54, 59, 61, 65–6, 69, 81–2
NLP study 157

One Life Live exhibition 143, 166
One Life Live survey 67, 86, 92, 114, 138
online marketing 58–60
online recruitment agencies 54
online services 20, 36, 40, 54, 119, 121, 124, 148, 166–8, 167
Open University 116, 133
open-minded thinking 9–10
opportunities 1, 2, 8
options 8–10, 35–6
outplacement companies 67
Overcoming Redundancy 167

paperwork 15–16
part-time work 8, 48, 56, 78–9, 114, 129, 134, 150–52

partnership 89–92
passion 75–7
patience 34
Penna 36, 166
personal image 102–4
pigeonholing 84
Plaxo 20, 148
portfolio career 150–52
positive thinking 1–3, 31–2, 45–6, 48, 82, 98, 159
priorities 99–101
professional advice 65
professional image coach 145
Professional Indemnity Insurance 88
psychometric tests 69
Public Liability Insurance 88

questions 33–4

reading 141–3, 158
reassessment 100–101
recruitment consultants 55–7, 82
Redundancy Counsellor 30–31
redundancy payment investment 71–4
Redundancy Transformation Study (2009) 2, 45–6, 68, 71, 100, 113, 120, 135, 136–7, 149, 153, 154
relatives 17–18, 124
relaxation 106
research 40–41, 64–6
retraining 2, 6, 11, 25, 27, 33, 35–8, 39–40, 55, 81, 111, 113, 122, 124, 130, 142, 145, 153, 243
roleplay technique 110
routines 125–7
Royal Bank of Scotland (RBS) 40, 124

school 132–4
self-belief 157–9
self-discipline 42
self-employment 21, 130

self-esteem 15, 24–6
shadowing 40
shopping habits 119
short-term work 78–9
skill audit 49–51
skill improvement 39–41
skills 24, 35, 66
Skills Venture 168
sleep and rest 16
slowing down 14
sole trading 86–8, 90
specialist recruitment consultants 54
startups 89–90
stepping stone approach 55–6, 78–9
stress 105–7
success 157–9
support group 147–9
survivor guilt 5

Teaching English as a Foreign Language (TEFL) 139
time 155–6
Time Banking 26, 167
training exchange 40
transition phase 107

university 132–4

vision 10, 113
visualisation technique 108–10, 112–13
Voluntary Services Overseas (VSO) 140, 168
voluntary work 25, 40, 42–4, 126

work abroad 138–40
working hours 129–30
workshops 87–8
The Writers Bureau 116
writing books 114–17

Yahoo Groups 59

Ziglar, Zig 142